Rearview-mirror packaging
Printed cardboard
11⁷⁄₈ x 9⁷⁄₈ x 9⁷⁄₈ in. (30 x 25 x 25 cm)
Mumbai, Jamshedji Petit Road, Grant Road, April 2003
The colors and the graphic style are as hard-hitting as the slogan, "The eye [represented by an illustration] at the back of your head," which asserts magical powers for the object. We suspect rearview mirrors have a decorative value that may equal their attraction as a safety accessory.

सफ़ाई सफ़ाई

धोना धोना

घिसना घिसना

झाड़ू लगाना झाड़ू लगाना

घिसना घिसना

चमकाना चमकाना

इस्त्री करना इस्त्री करना

ब्रुश ब्रुश

झाड़ू झाड़ू

पोछा पोछा

खुर्पी खुर्पी

बाल्टी बाल्टी

वाहन वाहन

Sweep — Iron — Polish — Brushes —

Bottle Brush — Dustpan — Housework

Housekeeping in India is very serious business. Indians battle dust and the deterioration caused by drought, monsoons, or insects, and wage a daily war on microbes. A caste of sweepers labors ceaselessly, and the whisper of leaves and branches against the earth, soft and monotonous, gives rhythm to the day. The diversity of brushes and brooms is staggering. The gleam of the bright colors household accessories generally bear seems to urge the indolent to get to work at once. These objects are easily found in every bazaar: Housework is a common preoccupation, a daily need, a permanent activity.

She knows that I cannot afford to lose my temper with her. It is difficult to find honest maidservants, and if she feels offended in any way, she will demand her wages and leave. So I control my tongue, although I long to comment on the way she sweeps the rooms in my apartment, the broom flicking across the floor, barely touching it, or the way she leaves a trail of damp after slapping a wet mop around, not even bothering to squeeze out the extra water. My helplessness infuriates Roopa and Kamini.

"Why don't you get rid of the rotten woman?" shouts Kamini across the phone line.

"Because the next one I find might be worse."

Anita Rau Badami, *Tamarind Woman*
Chapel Hill, NC: Algonquin Books, 2002

Scrub — Broom — Bucket — Dustpan

Pitchers and brush
Plastic
Pitcher: 5^1/$_2$ x 5^1/$_2$ in. (14 x 14 cm)
Brush: 5^3/$_8$ x 1^3/$_4$ x 1^3/$_8$ in. (13.5 x 4.5 x 3.5 cm)
Delhi, Lajpat Nagar, October 2003

Bucket
Injection-molded plastic
12^1/4 x 13 in. (31 x 33 cm)
Mumbai, Chor Bazaar, February 1999

Three brushes
Wood, plastic bristles
7 7/8 x 2–2 3/8 x 2 in. (20 x 5–6 x 5 cm)
Mumbai, Null Bazaar, April 2003
These thick brushes in attractive colors are used for domestic chores in the home, such as scrubbing floors.

Brush
Wood, bristles of recycled plastic
5 1/8 x 2 x 2 1/8 in. (13 x 5 x 5.3 cm)
Mumbai, Chor Bazaar, April 2003
The subtle variation in the colors of the recycled plastic bristles, set in a rudimentary block of wood,
attracted us to this brush.

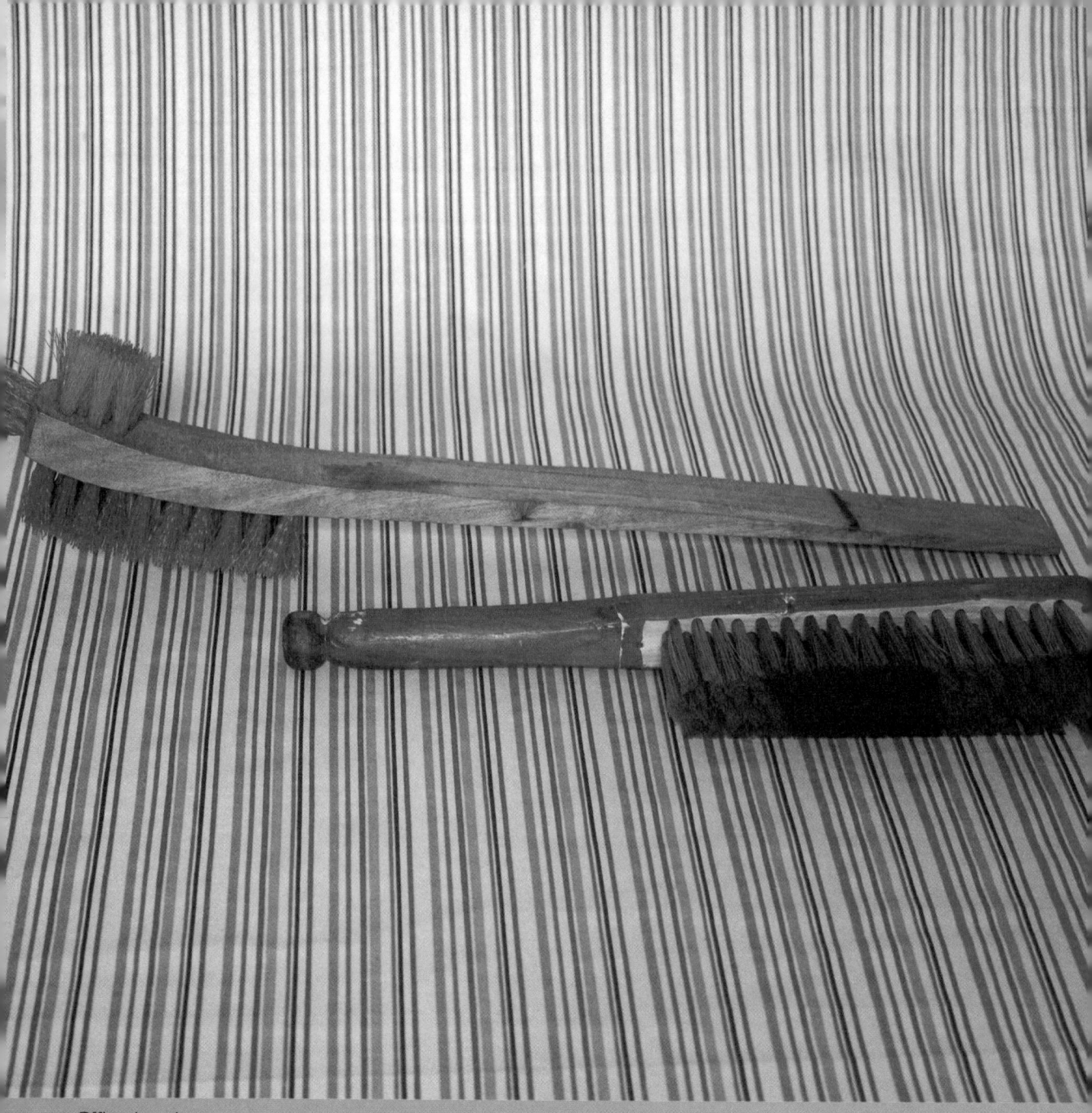

Office brushes
Wood, dyed coconut fiber
19 1/8 x 3 1/2 x 1 3/4 in. (48.5 x 9 x 4.5 cm)
Mumbai, Null Bazaar, April 2003
What can we say about this remarkable shape?

Feather duster/brush
Plastic
35 ³/₈ x 2 ³/₈ in. (90 x 6 cm)
Mumbai, Null Bazaar, April 2003
Feather dusters and brushes are accessories of the utmost importance, both in the home and in shops or in front of various buildings. First, one of the most widespread activities throughout the day consists of administering a regular dusting or sweeping to the interior and exterior perimeters of shops. Sometimes, the goal of this operation seems to be more to raise the dust (to stir it up a little from time to time) than to eliminate it. Dust in India is an endlessly present subject, seeming to have its own density—a particular density that, undisturbed by vacuum cleaners, allows it to remain wherever it is undisturbed.

Scouring pads
Plastic
2 3/4 x 1 3/8 in. (7 x 3.5 cm)
Jodhpur, February 2001
This batch of scouring pads sports a remarkable combination of colors.

Bottle brush
Iron wire and nylon
15 3/4 x 2 in. (40 x 5 cm)
Mumbai, Null Bazaar, April 2003
This handsome bottle brush, despite the menial tasks it is designed for, does not hesitate to dress itself
in the colors of the national flag.

Clothing brushes
Plastic
5 3/8 x 1 3/4 x 1 3/8 in. (13.5 x 4.5 x 3.5 cm)
Jaipur, Tripolia Bazaar, January 1999
These plastic brushes are sold as a set in a striking assortment. They are used for doing laundry by
hand. In India, it is usual to give dirty laundry to a *dhobbi*, who takes it away and brings it back a few
days later, washed and ironed. Few households own washing machines.

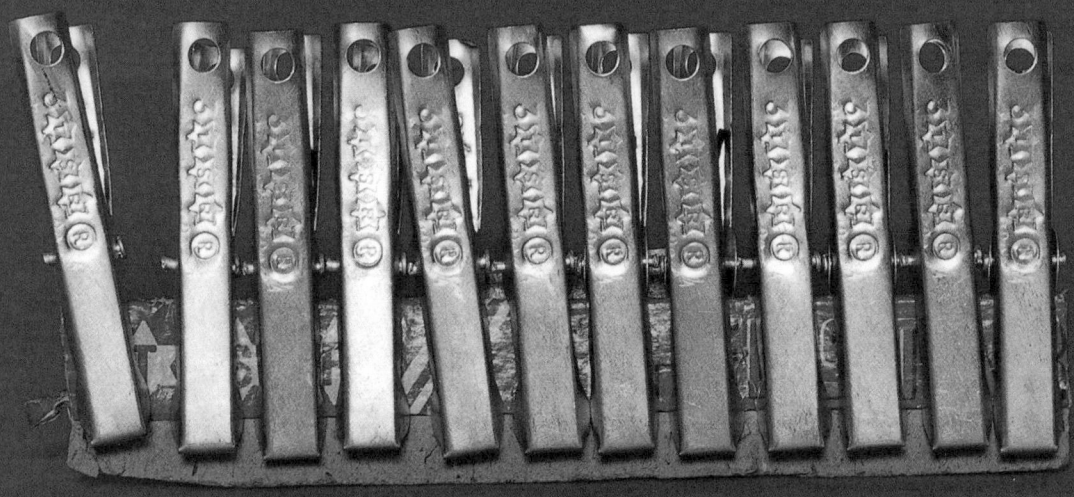

Clothespins
Aluminum
2 3/4 x 3/8 in. (7 x 1 cm)
Jaipur, Tripolia Bazaar, February 2001
These clothespins were once very popular, but they are now becoming increasingly rare as they are
replaced by plastic ones. All the same, aluminum does not rust.

Electric iron
Painted metal, speckled finish
8 1/2 x 4 3/8 x 4 1/8 in. (21.5 x 11 x 10.5 cm)
Mumbai, Chor Bazaar, February 1999
The electric iron is certainly a genuine symbol of domestic progress. This one, triumphantly decorated, has a particularly aerodynamic shape and is incredibly light. The small size and the precision of the speckled finish provide good camouflage: This finish is typical of small-scale, local production.

Electric iron
Metal painted in two colors, plastic
7 7/8 x 4 3/4 x 4 3/8 in. (20 x 12 x 11 cm)
Mumbai, Chor Bazaar, February 1999
Not too long ago, it was common to use heavy irons filled with red-hot coals, like those still used in street laundries. The first "modern" models, from which this one is descended, were still rather heavy, and retained the massive look of their ancestors.

Locking faucet
Metal
3 3/8 x 2 3/8 in. (8.5 x 6 cm)
Bangalore, February 1999
These faucets are unusual in that they can be locked, thus denying access to water to anyone who doesn't have a key—a common way to protect property in India. This type is often used by shopkeepers, who want to prevent everybody from being able to use the faucet outside the shop.

Faucet
Plated plastic
4 3/8 x 4 3/8 in. (11 x 11 cm)
Jaipur, Tripolia Bazaar, January 2001
These plastic faucets are not used as household implements, but are, instead, attached to street
peddlers' large metal water cans or screwed to water containers in the shantytowns. In kitchens, they
are placed on potbellied water jars or on cans furnished with a filter.

Pale pink faucet
Plastic and metal
$3\,^7/_8$ x $4\,^1/_2$ in. (10 x 11.5 cm)
Bangalore, February 1999

Bright pink faucet
Plastic
$3\,^1/_2$ x $4\,^3/_8$ in. (9 x 11 cm)
Bangalore, February 1999

Small pink faucet
Plastic
$2\,^1/_8$ x $3\,^7/_8$ in.
(5.3 x 10 cm)
Delhi, January 2001

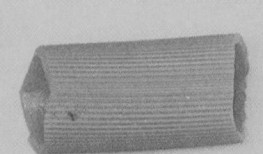

Blue faucet
Plastic
$3\,^7/_8$ x $4\,^3/_4$ in.
(10 x 12 cm)
Bangalore, February 1999

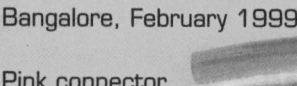

Pink connector
Plastic
$4\,^1/_8$ x 1 in. (10.5 x 2.6 cm)
Bangalore, February 1999

Grooved tubing
Plastic
$1\,^3/_8$ in. (diameter)
(3.6 cm)
Delhi, January 2001

Pink tubing
Plastic
1 in. (diameter) (2.6 cm)
Delhi, January 2001

Purple tubing
Plastic
$^5/_8$ in. (diameter)
(1.6 cm)
Delhi, January 2001

This assortment allows an appreciation of the variety
of colors and forms available in tubing, depending on
the mode of production: Every small manufacturer
has complete control over material and design.

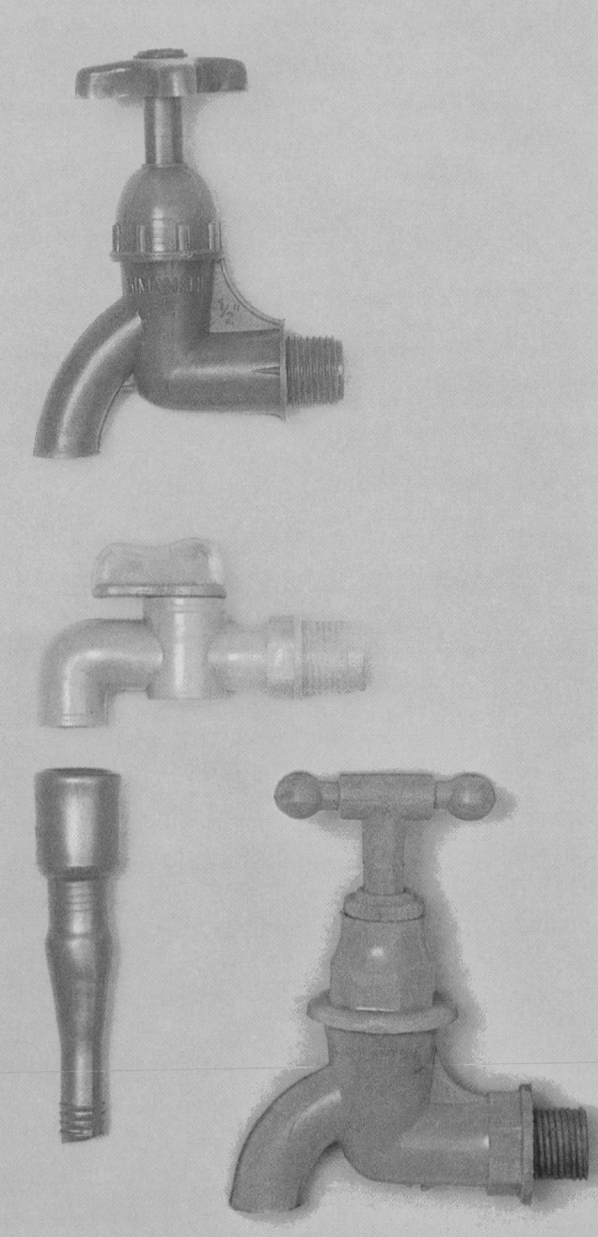

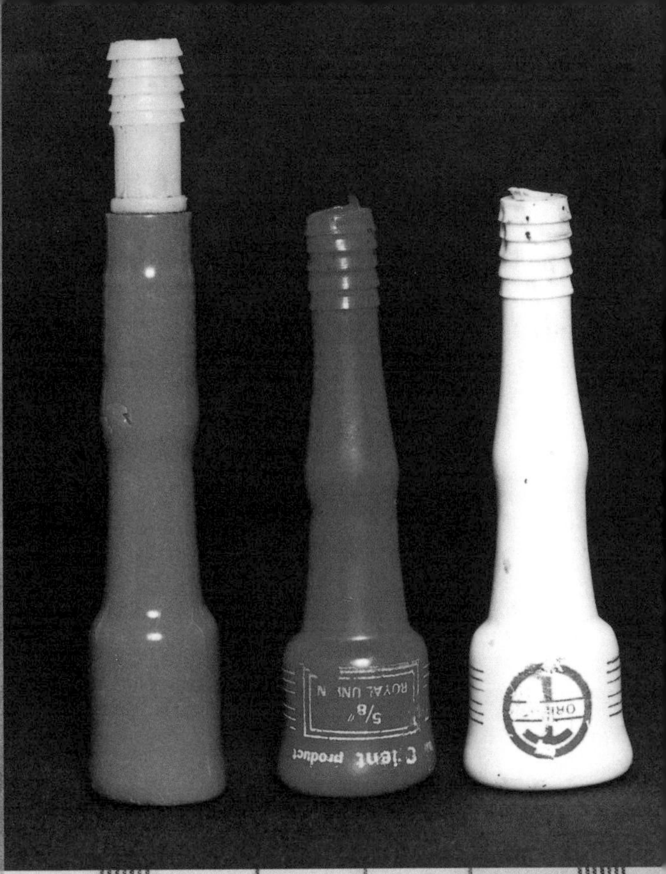

Tubing connectors
Thick, iridescent plastic
3 1/2 x 1 1/8 in. (diameter) (9 x 3 cm)
Bangalore, February 1999

Tubing connectors
Thick, matte-finished plastic
3 1/2 x 1 1/8 in. (diameter) (9 x 3 cm)
Jaipur, Nehru Bazaar, February 1999

Tubing connectors
Flexible, iridescent plastic
3 1/2 x 1 1/8 in. (diameter) (9 x 3 cm)
Bangalore, February 1999

Water in India is rarely available throughout
the whole day, and interruptions in service
are frequent. People often use a length of
tubing every morning to fill various containers
to hold water for cooking or cleaning. These
objects are employed to attach the tubing to
the faucet.

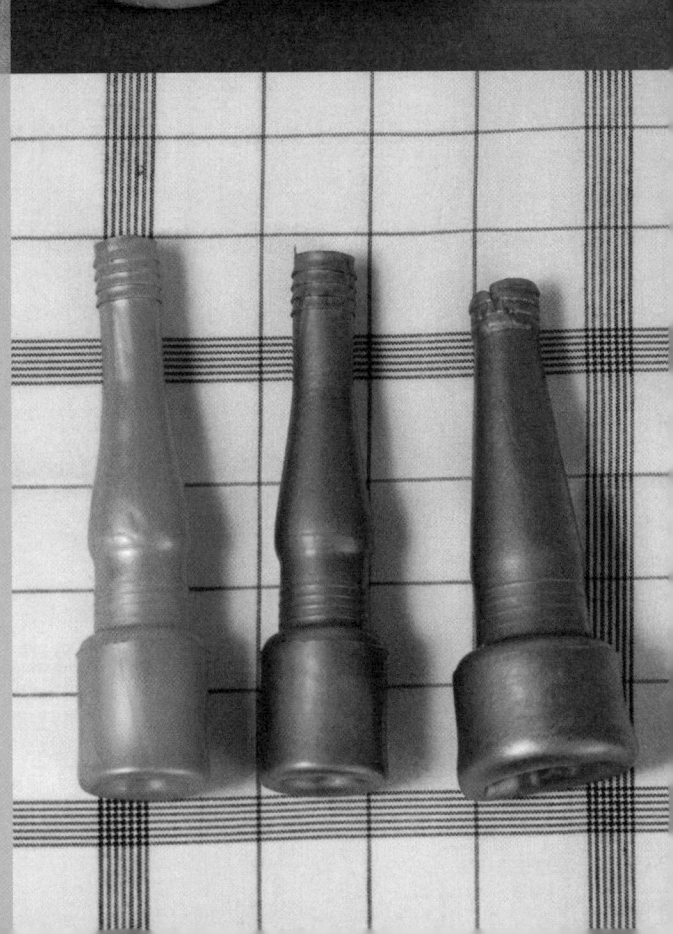

Dustpans
Embossed stainless steel
9 7/8 x 7 1/8 in. (25 x 18 cm)
Mumbai, Null Bazaar, April 2003
Dustpans in India are rather smaller than those common in the United States. Their size suggests precision work.

Dustpan
Brightly colored plastic
9 7/8 x 7 1/4 in. (25 x 18.5 cm)
Mumbai, Null Bazaar, April 2003
These dustpans come with brushes, bowls, and buckets made of the same materials.

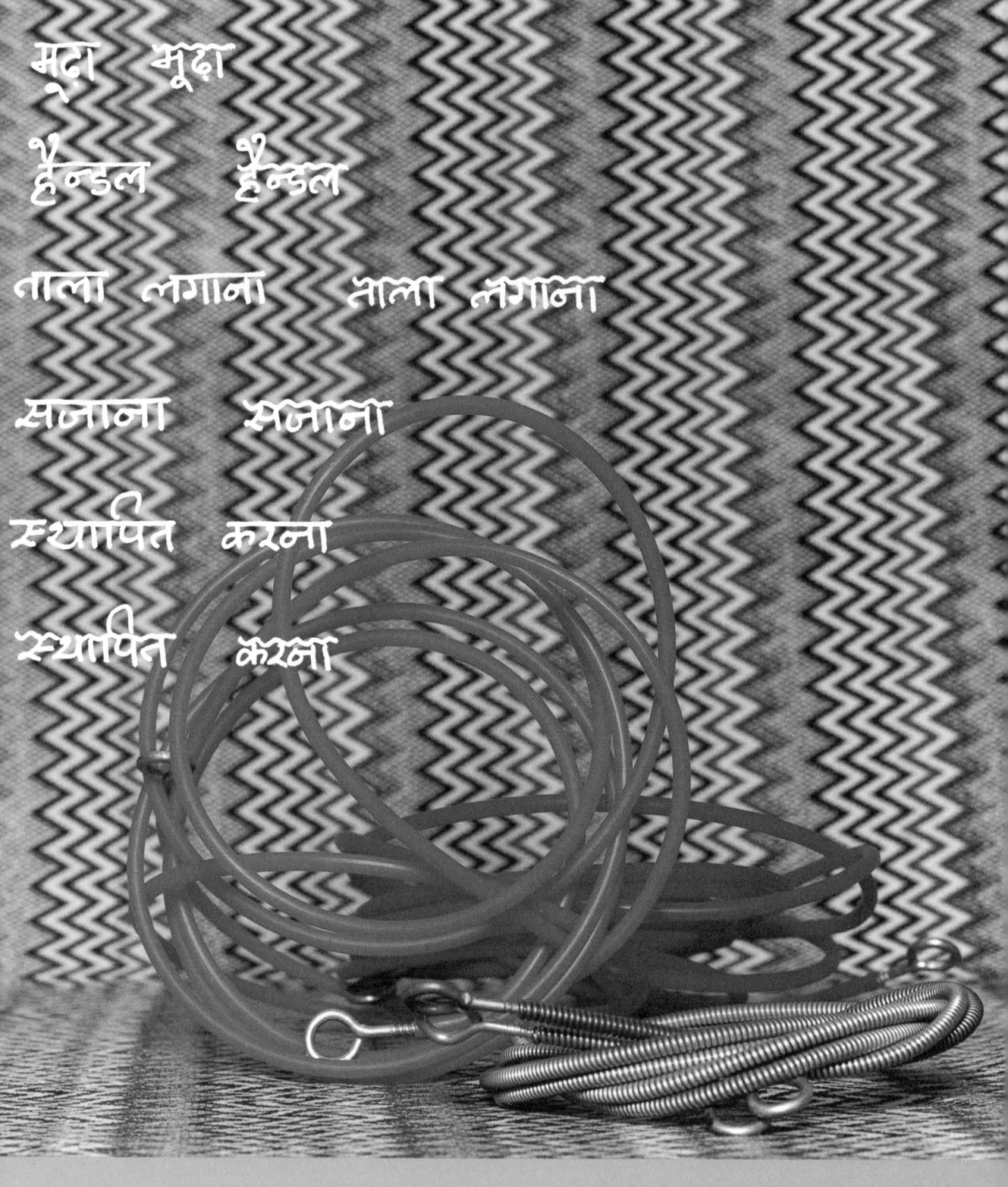

मूढ़ा मूढ़ा

हैन्डल हैन्डल

ताला लगाना ताला लगाना

सजाना सजाना

स्थापित करना

स्थापित करना

Close — Organize — Stretch Out —

Sit — Hang — Settle In

Furnishings are rather sparse in Indian homes, and furniture is generally modest. Even if the elements vary enormously from one home to another, some of them—a curtain, a trunk locked with a padlock, a *charpoy* (a hammock-like bed), a doorknob, a footstool—are part of the essentials, and are enumerated in many versions.

Mirror, razor, shaving brush, plastic cup, loata, copper water pot—Ishvar arranged them on an upturned cardboard carton in one corner of the shack. Trunk and bedding took up most of the remaining space. He hung their clothes from rusted nails protruding through the plywood walls. "So everything fits nicely. We have jobs, we have a house, and soon we'll find a wife for you."

Om did not smile. "I hate this place," he said.

Rohinton Mistry, *A Fine Balance*
New York: Vintage, 1997

Air — Display — Padlock — Strap

Fan store
Mumbai, Saifee Jubilee Street, April 2003
This shop, which specializes in fans, is a good demonstration of the life cycle of goods in India. Everything is repaired, overhauled, fixed up. For either salvage or recycling, stores are usually stocked with all the

parts necessary to repair, and even improve, appliances. Everything is taken apart. Anything really beyond repair is stripped, and the carcasses are carefully stored for reuse. This is a kind of physical reincarnation and economic enlightenment.

Padlocks
Painted steel
2–2 3/8 x 3/8–1/2 in. (5–6 cm x 1–1.3 cm)
Jaipur, 1999; Mumbai, 2003
Padlocks exist in every size and in all colors, and in every quality as well. Each, even the most diminutive, has something to protect from lurking thieves. Many family members often share living spaces, and jealousy and pilfering are, as anywhere else in the world, quite common. Treasures are locked up in iron boxes, in sheet-metal trunks—even telephones, faucets, or electric lightbulbs may be padlocked. The abundance of displays devoted to sales and repair of this article demonstrates its popularity.

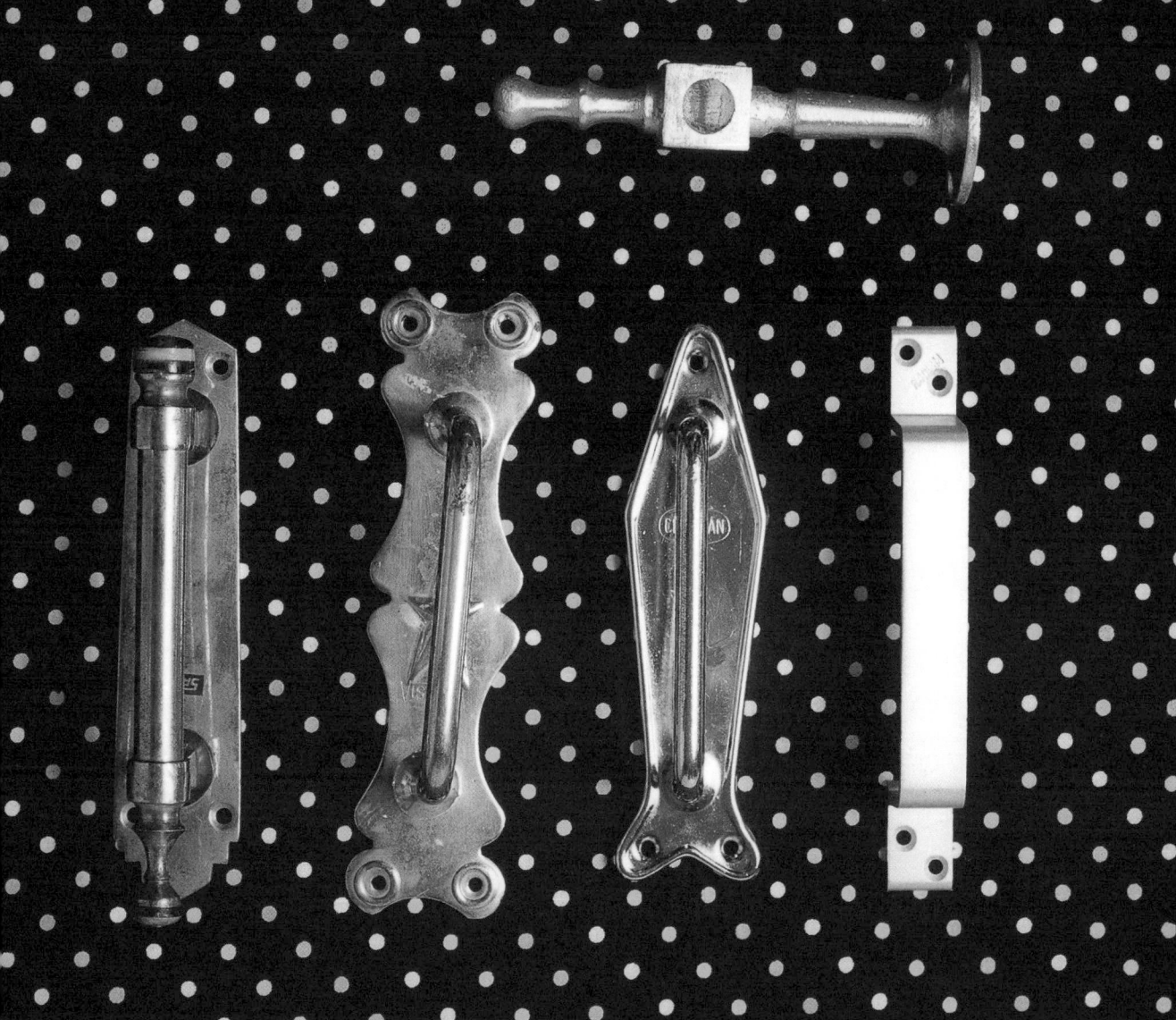

Door pulls
Aluminum, stainless steel, iron, plastic
5 1/8–5 7/8 in. (13–15 cm)

Vendors selling door pulls, hardware, coat pegs, and curtain rods are highly visible in Indian bazaars, and seem prosperous. It seems residents strive to stand out from the neighbors by the spectacle of the front-door pull, and this article is imbued with a special significance. Manufacturers don't need to tie up a lot of material in these objects, and this is why we often find pieces that are original—to say the least—products of local manufacture. The variety available is very broad, aimed at every taste and every pocketbook. Also, closets in India are often simply alcoves hollowed into the wall and closed by wooden doors furnished with pulls, hence the magnitude of the market.

The counters of street shops, selling *chai* (tea with spices and milk), *bidis* (cigarettes made from a tree leaf rolled around pieces of tobacco), *paan* (a sweet mixture of lime paste, cardamom, fennel, honey, areca nut, and, often though not always, flavored tobacco, all wrapped in a betel leaf), or sugarcane juice, are often surrounded by a low metal barrier, a symbolic antitheft device from which merchandise is hung. This railing, which demarcates the boundary between inside and outside the store, is held in place by pieces of aluminum fixed in the wooden surface of the counter, like the one seen resting horizontally in this photograph.

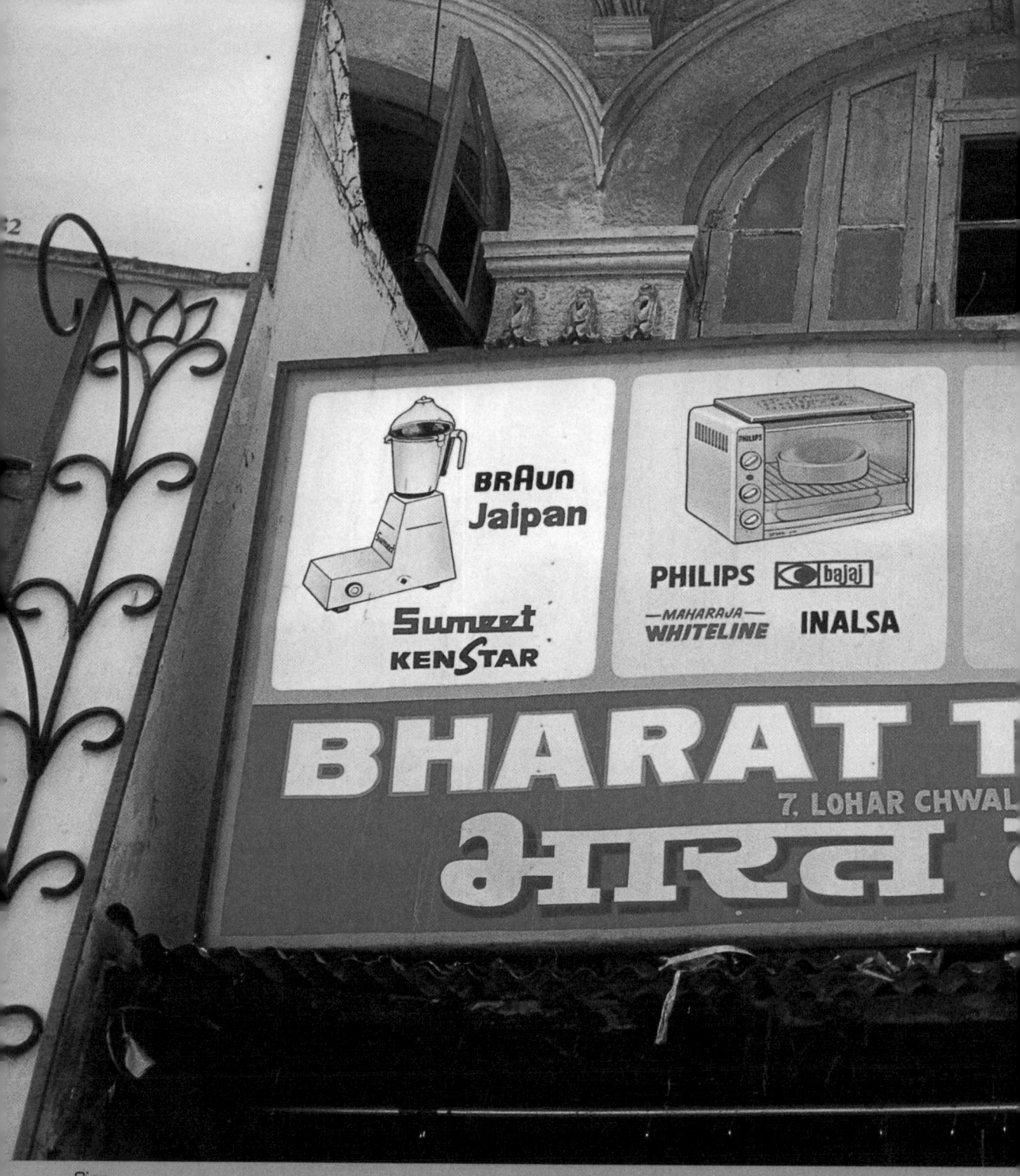

Sign
Painted metal
Mumbai, Lohar Chawl, April 2003
This sign conveys its essential information at a glance: "Bharat Traders." In the shadow of a handsome
residence, an Indian merchant sells Indian products. Through the sign painters' skill, we see the faithful

reproduction of mixers, ovens, or fans: These relatively unattractive objects seem to bow politely, ready to do their duty with solemnity. Although Western- or Japanese-sounding brand names (Braun, Philips, Jaipan) are listed, all these products were designed and manufactured in India.

Ashtrays
Stainless steel, Bakelite, anodized aluminum
$1\,5/8 \times 2\,3/8$ in. (diameter) (4 x 6 cm)
Mumbai, Mohamed Ali and Kalbadevi roads, April 2003
The familiar shape of these ashtrays is reproduced in varying sizes and various materials. Their presence signifies that one is in a place where one should not drop ashes and cigarette butts on the ground. They mark a certain affluence, because they are needed only for Western cigarettes, whose prestige is much higher than that of the traditional *bidis,* which certainly don't need any help going out.

Footstools
Stainless steel
10 3/8 x 10 3/8 in. (diameter) (26.5 x 26.5 cm)
Mumbai, Kalbadevi Road, April 2003

Recycled painted steel
13 3/4 x 9 7/8 in. (diameter) (35 x 25 cm)
Jaipur, February 2001

Painted fiberglass and resin
16 1/2 x 16 1/2 x 16 1/2 in. (42 x 42 x 42 cm)
Delhi, February 2003

Straps
Woven nylon
2–2 1/2 in. (5–6.5 cm)
Jaipur, February 1999; Nawalgarh, February 2002; Mumbai, Mohamed Ali Road, April 2003
These straps are mainly used to make *charpoys*. They're stretched over a wooden frame that serves as box springs and mattress. In the summer, when it's very hot, many people prefer to sleep outside on these beds.

Corners
Stamped aluminum, folded and anodized
$1\,^1/_8$ x 1 x $^3/_8$ in. (3 x 2.5 x 1 cm)
Jaipur, Tripolia Bazaar, February 2001
Picture framers fasten these corners to the angles of the many portraits of ancestors, divinities, and gurus put under glass to protect them from the voracity of insects and the humidity of the monsoon. Mirrors, often made to measure, are also supplied with these little accessories, which give them a finishing touch—in color, should you so desire.

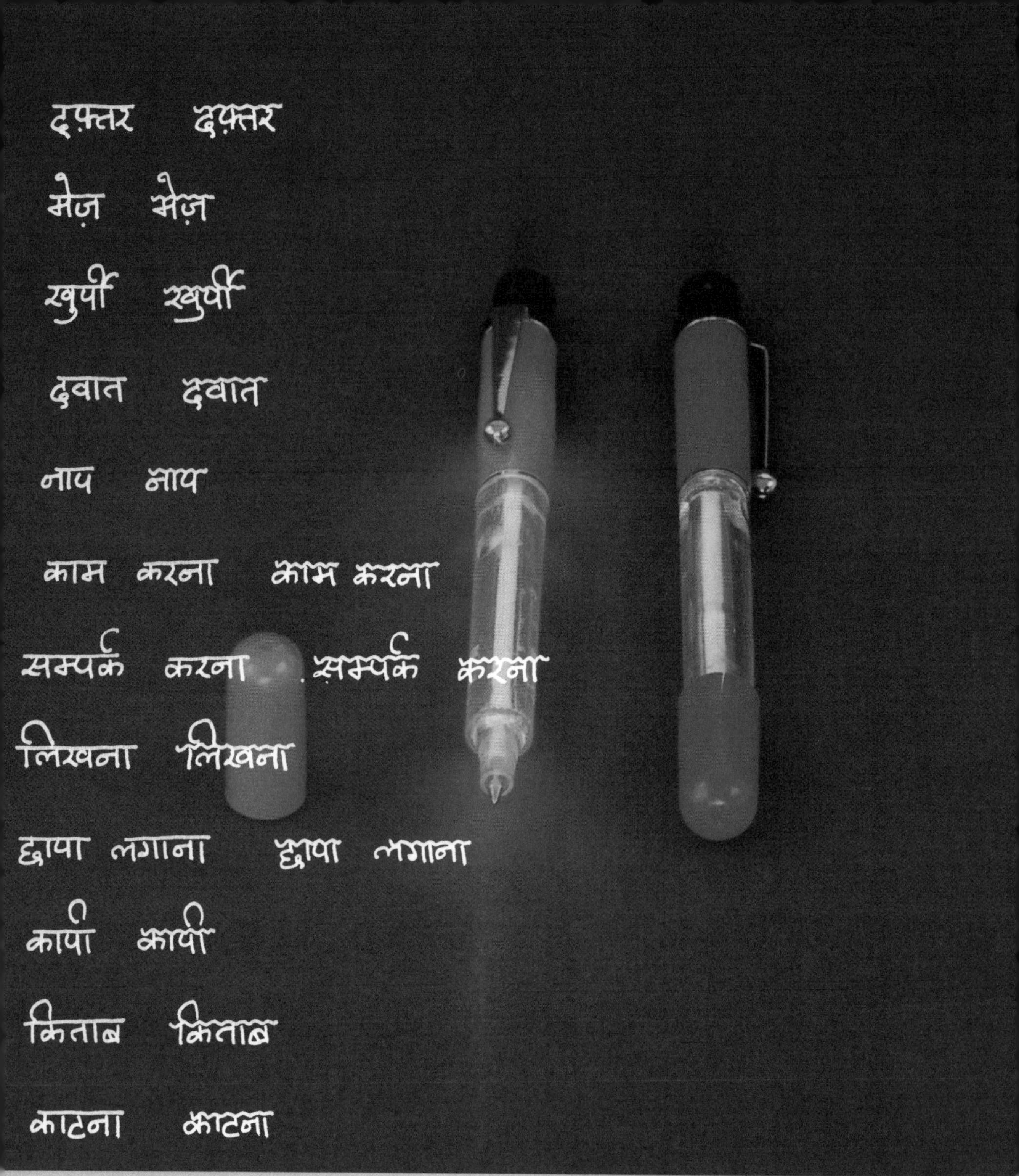

दफ़्तर दफ़्तर

मेज़ मेज़

खुर्पी खुर्पी

दवात दवात

नाव नाव

काम करना काम करना

सम्पर्क करना सम्पर्क करना

लिखना लिखना

छापा लगाना छापा लगाना

कॉपी कॉपी

किताब किताब

काटना काटना

Office — Measure — Work — Write —

Registers — Cut — Make

Professional implements, equipment, and accessories, and all the stationery of the office, are holy in Indian eyes. Studying is a luxury; work, an opportunity. These objects have prestige, provide comforts, open doors. In the Hindu religious calendar, the feast of Vishwakarma honors the creator of the world by a series of rituals: Students lay their textbooks at the feet of the goddess Saraswati, businessmen start new account books, and, especially, workers and artisans clean their machines, coat them with sandalwood and vermilion powder, and let them rest all day long. These days, this practice extends to computers: Garlands of flowers hang from their screens, and prayer incense burns on their keyboards.

Ibrahim was an elderly man but looked old beyond his years. In his left hand . . . he carried a plastic folder secured by two large rubber bands. . . . The folder handed down almost a half a century ago by the retiring rent collector had not been of plastic, but rudely fashioned out of two wooden boards bound by a strip of morocco. It had carried with it the previous owner's smell. . . .Then, on one lucky day, the morocco spine broke. . . . After a fortnight's delay, the new folder arrived. It was built of buck-ramed cardboard, very smart and modern-looking, in colour a dignified umber. Ibrahim was delighted.

Rohinton Mistry, *A Fine Balance*
New York: Vintage, 1997

Communicate — Stamp

Pliers and shears
Steel and plastic
4 3/4 x 1 5/8–7 7/8 x 2 3/4 in. (12 x 4 cm–20 x 7 cm)
Jaipur, February 1999; Jodhpur, February 2001; Mumbai, Ghandji Street, April 2003
These tools may be purchased from street peddlers, displays in the street, bazaar stalls, or more specialized stores—those that sell jewelers' supplies, for example. Wrapped in a thick layer of protective grease, these tools are remarkable for their range of quality: They're forged by hand, and their performance varies; the buyer must beware. Those that look most refined—whose handles are encased in plastic, for example—are not necessarily the best designed or best made; the precision of form of even the crudest among them is remarkable. They're carefully maintained, and they may always be sharpened and repaired, even improved, by the artisan who owns them. They're sometimes sold by the pound in village bazaars.

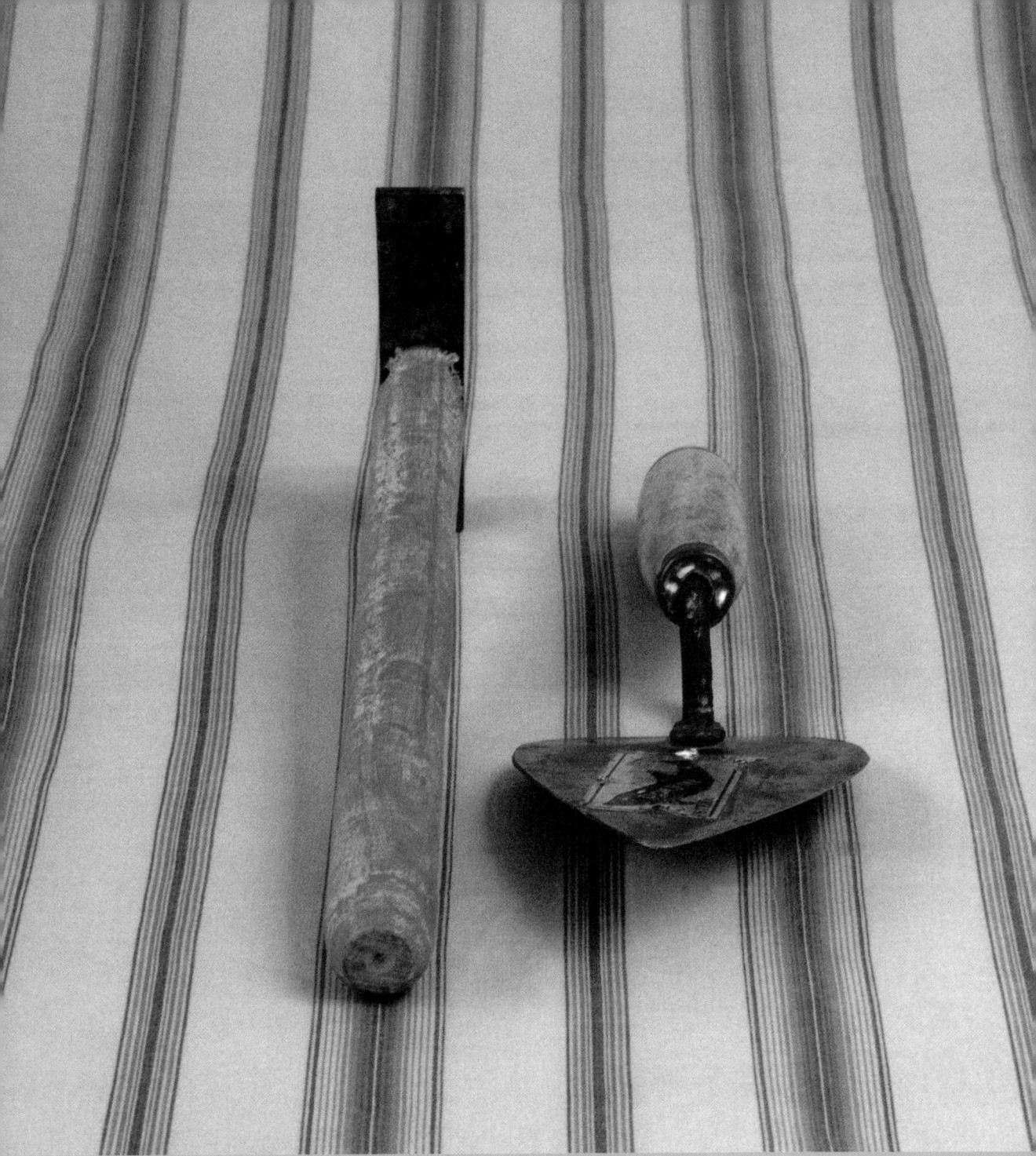

Trowel and hammer
Wood and metal
Trowel: 9 x 2 ³/₄ in. (23 x 7 cm)
Hammer: 10 ¹/₄ x 3 ¹/₈ in. (26 x 8 cm)
Jaipur, January 1999
These tools are inexpensive, but, despite a rather crude finish, their handles are decorated with thin
lines of red, orange, and green paint.

Pincers
Painted steel
6 1/4 x 1 3/4 in. (16 x 4.5 cm)
Jaipur, January 1999

Measuring tape
Plastic-impregnated cloth, plastic, metal
3 $^7/_8$ in. (diameter) (10 cm)
Bangalore, February 1999
This tool's impressive size is due to its great capacity: It can measure up to around 25 feet (7.5 meters). The tape, a smart orange color, is graduated in centimeters on one side and inches on the other, but the printing, which appears to have been stenciled on, leaves a little room for error. The tape can be rewound by a little folding handle. The textured plastic of the cover imitates leather, giving its owner a certain prestige, and the tape claims to be made of metal, but doesn't keep its word: It is plasticized cloth.

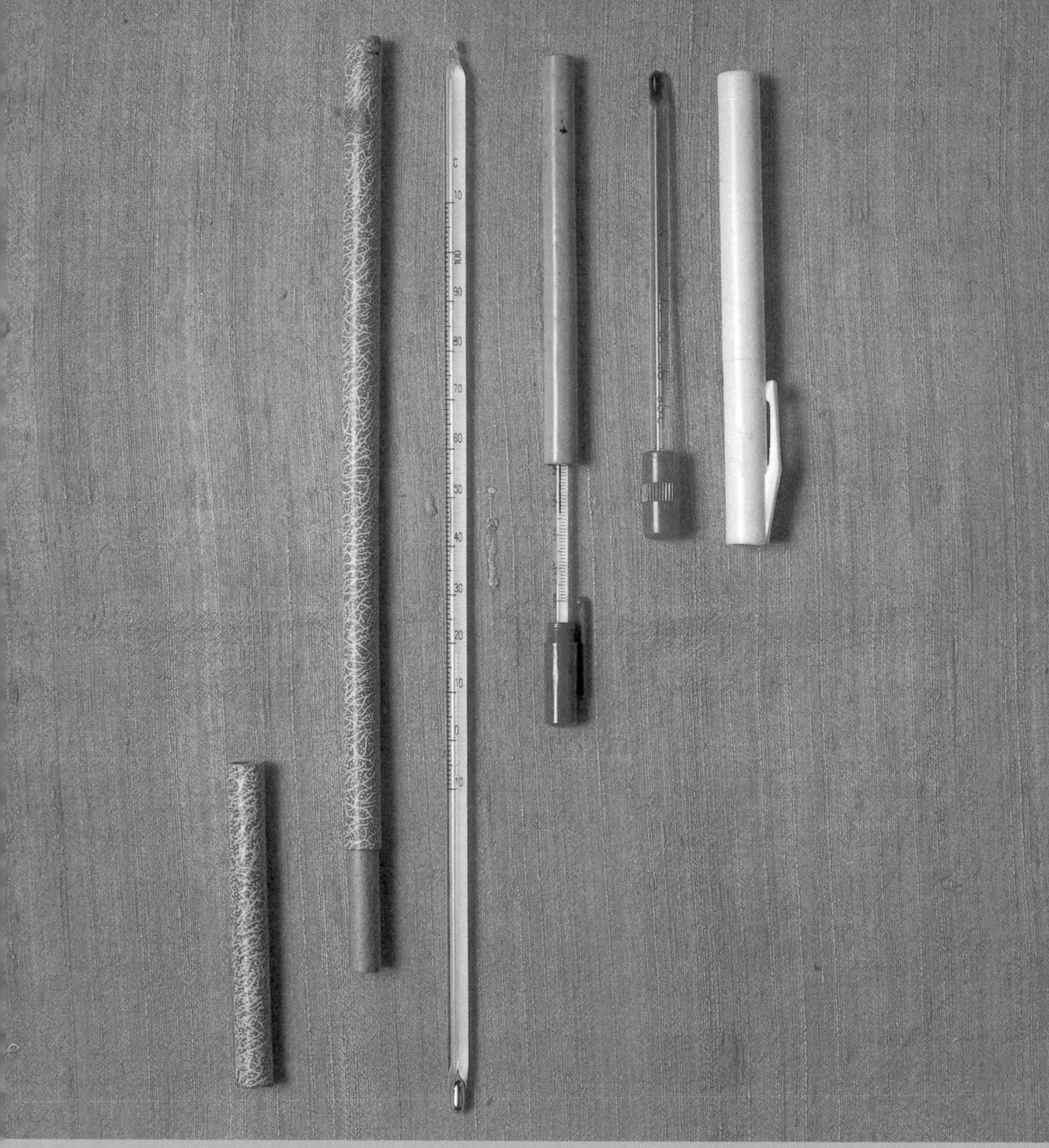

Thermometers
Glass, colored alcohol, mercury, plastic
Mumbai, April 2003
5 7/8–12 5/8 x 1/4 in. (15–32 cm x 0.7 cm)
The first two thermometers from the right are for household use; one may be nattily worn clipped to a pocket, like a pen. The third from the right is for more technical use; it reads up to 212 degrees Fahrenheit (100 degrees Celsius).

Funnel with integral filter
Porcelain
3 x 4 $^7/_8$ in. (7.5 x 12.5 cm)
Mumbai, April 2003
This handsome filter is doubtless designed for laboratory use. Its beveled end, which produces a
constant flow, acts as a filter; it is suited to all kinds of corrosive products.

Measuring cup
Enameled steel
3 1/2 x 5 1/8 x 6 3/4 in. (9 x 13 x 17 cm)
Mumbai, April 2003
This measuring cup is probably for professional use, because enamelware is rather expensive in India; it is highly resistant to acids. However, the carelessness with which the enamel is applied where the handle is attached contrasts with the precision of the graduation.

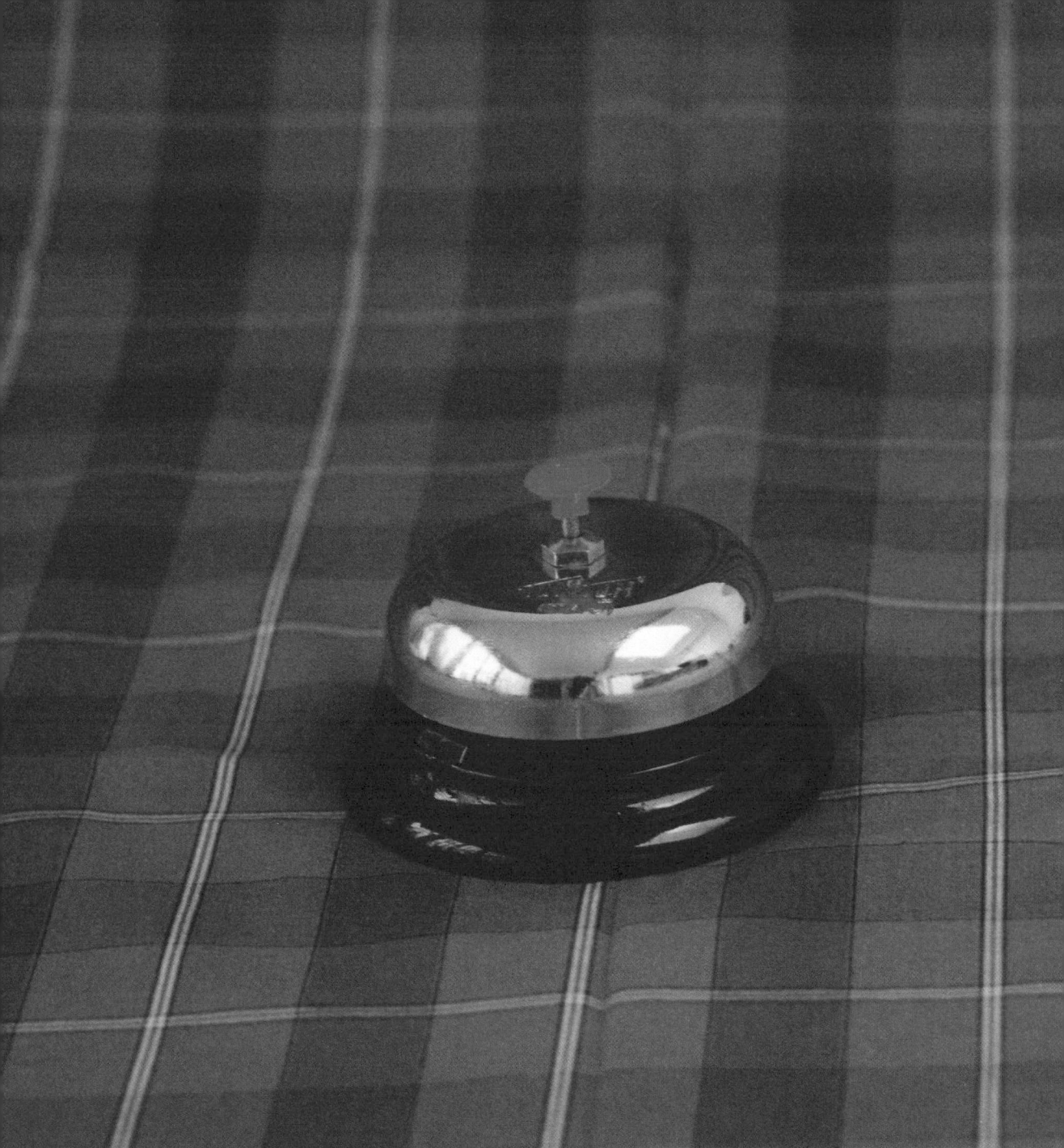

Call bell
Stainless steel and plastic
3 1/2 x 2 3/8 in. (9 x 6 cm)
Mumbai, Kalbadevi Road, April 2003
The sight of this solemn instrument immediately provokes the irresistible urge to give it a good
smack with the flat of the hand and make it ring loudly. In offices and other institutions, the boss
uses it to summon his employees so they can bring him an important file—or the indispensable
chai that punctuates the days.

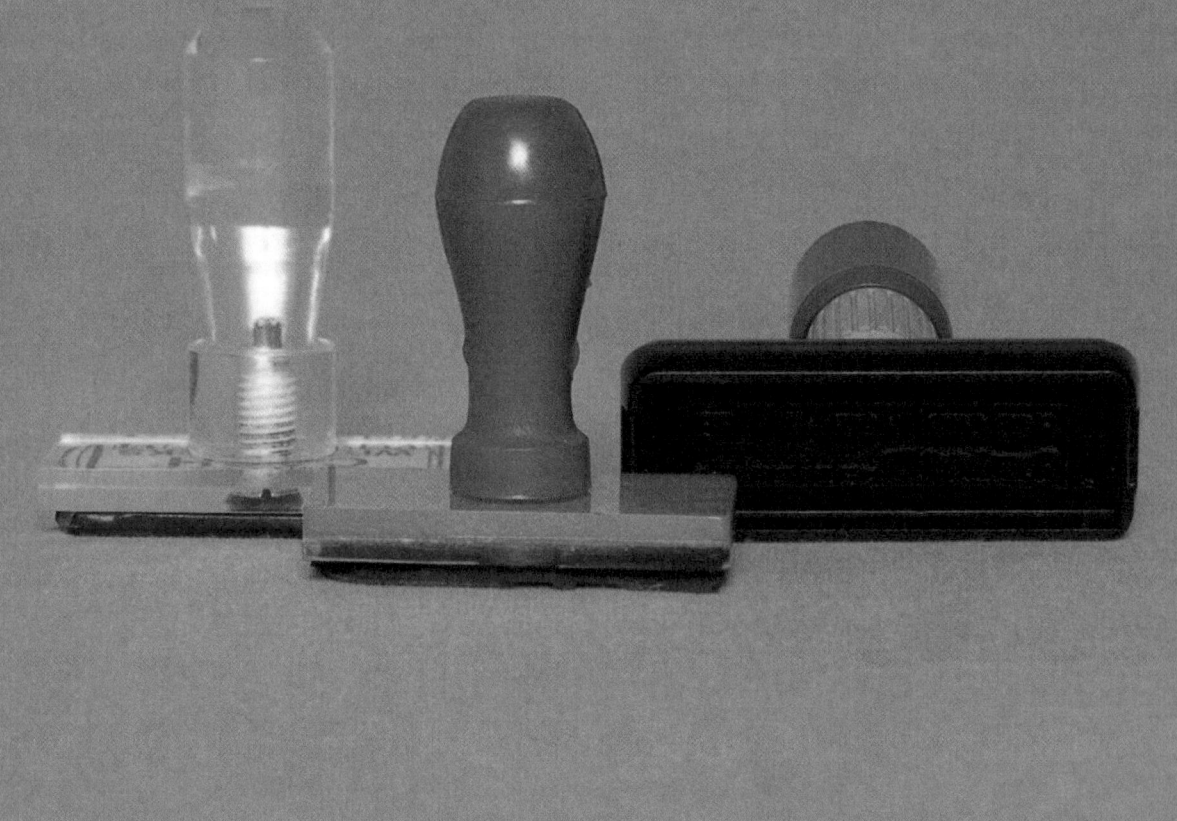

Rubber stamps
Plastic, rubber
2–2 5/8 x 1 7/8–2 in. (5.2–6.8 cm x 4.9–5.2 cm)
Mumbai, Kalbadevi Road, April 2003
Anyone who has traveled in India has surely noticed the great number of rubber stamps used on every
occasion in the course of a day, little thumps that mark an end to all sorts of transactions: purchases,
registration, paying a toll, and so on. This item punctuates daily life with little moments of sonorous

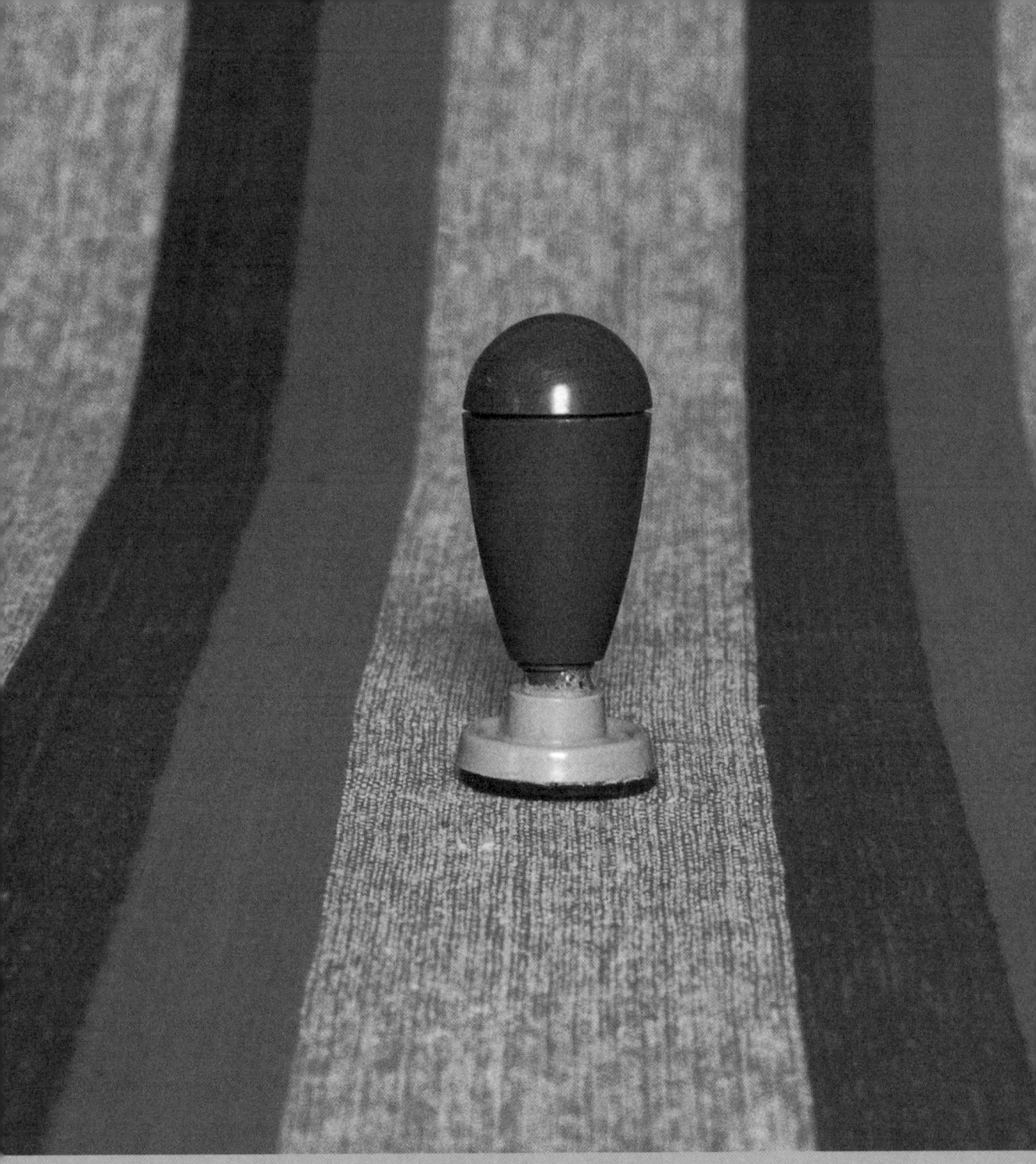

pleasure and is essential to anyone seriously established in business. Sometimes, you find yourself trying to evaluate the social rank of the person you are dealing with by the number and sizes of the stamps displayed on his or her desk. The archetypal stamp, in the past, was invariably black and orange. Nowadays, however, they are made of plastic and may be of any color, or might even be transparent—a sign of order and clarity.

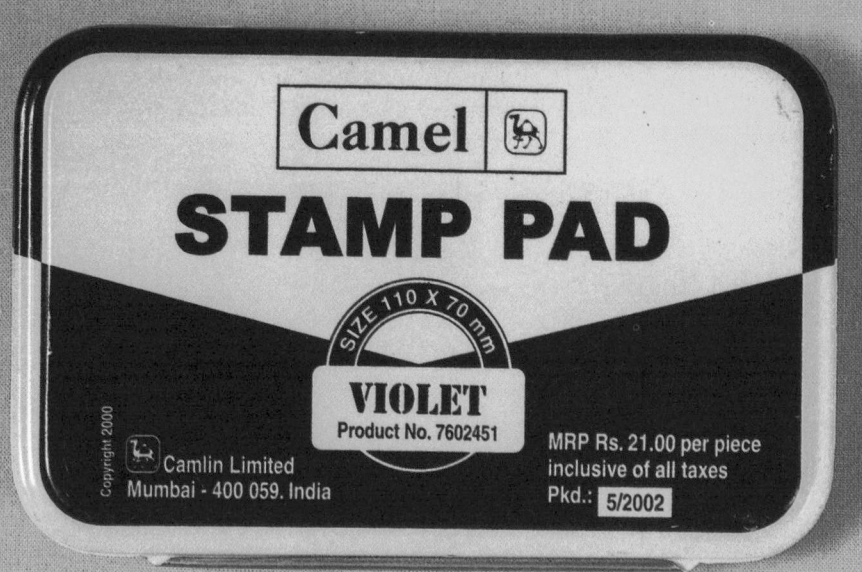

Stamp pad
Ink, foam rubber, metal
4 3/8 x 2 1/2 in. (11 x 6.5 cm)
Mumbai, Kalbadevi Road, April 2003
The Camel brand is well known in India, especially around Mumbai, for office and school supplies.

Locking telephone
Plastic, metal, wire
7 1/8 x 7 7/8 x 3 3/4 in. (18 x 20 x 9.5 cm)
Mumbai, Chor Bazaar, 1999
This lock reveals how doggedly Indians are forced to defend their possessions in quarters often shared by many people. Attached to the telephone, it emphasizes the importance of the apparatus and discourages dishonest profiteers, though it apparently does not keep Hindu deities Radha and Krishna from communicating with each other.

Boss notebook
Paper and cardboard
7 1/2 x 5 7/8 x 5/8 in. (19 x 15 x 1.5 cm)
Jaipur, February 1999
This notebook, with a style very common in the bazaars, claims to elevate whoever possesses it to an enviable status. As an added attraction, its edge is decorated with bright colors.

Clipboard
Stainless steel
5 1/2 x 8 1/4 in. (14 x 21 cm)
Mumbai, April 2003
Indispensable to every schoolchild, student, office employee, or salesperson, this device tightly holds sheets of paper to a metal plate. Sometimes aluminum, sometimes stainless steel, it keeps pages from being blown about by the ubiquitous office fan and, especially, provides a smooth and uniform writing surface for careful preparation of copies and other forms. Wooden tables and desks are often deeply furrowed, and writing on such tortuous surfaces is rather difficult.

Hand clip
Tin
3 1/8 x 2 in. (8 x 5 cm)
Calcutta, Auction House, February 2002
The little tin hand also holds any papers that might blow away. It rests on a table but also may be attached to a wall.

Assorted notebooks
Paper, cardboard, string, and cloth
8 1/4 x 6 3/4 in. (21 x 17 cm), varying thicknesses
Jaipur, February 1999; Ajmer, 2001; Mumbai, April 2003
Exercise books, account books, and notebooks come in a great number of sizes and colors, lined or unlined. The oversewn red style is typical of Rajasthan. The color of the cloth is invariable, but the thread may be red or white. They are used as account books, and every shop has similar notebooks piled up on its shelves. Some feature pages with printed or slightly embossed lines.

Envelopes
Paper
3 7/8–8 1/4 x 2 3/4–5 7/8 in. (10–21 x 7–15 cm)
Jodhpur, February 2001; Jaipur, February 2003; Mumbai, April 2003
Indians write often; many of them have a family member who lives on the other side of the country or abroad. Envelopes follow the rule of limitless choice: They may be found in every color and in all sizes, and for all occasions. Administrative or professional envelopes are white and usually lined with violet, and they are very heavy, thus resistant to mishaps such as tearing, wrinkling, and spills. Envelopes for marriage invitations are very thick, with a great deal of red and gilt illustration, embossed portraits of divinities, and a little string to fasten them, traditionally with sealing wax. There is an envelope for money given on various occasions, such as on the feast day of Divali, the envelope for which is decorated with a one-rupee piece.

Bags of rubber bands
Synthetic rubber
3/4–1 5/8 in. (diameter) (2–4 cm)
Jaipur, February 1999; Mumbai, Kalbadevi Road, April 2003
The national infatuation with rubber bands is evidence of the worth attached to every object, to every piece of merchandise. They are used to knot, to tie, to hold, to protect. They seal plastic bags hermetically for protection from the monsoon's humidity and sometimes replace string to wrap packets of paper. They are not wasted, however, because they are precious. Indian creativity manages to reveal itself even in this restricted medium: Rubber bands are fluorescent, multicolored, wide, thick, little. The three-colored style has replaced a two-colored one, and, even in this realm, the search for novelty is in full swing. Black rubber bands, often of irregular thickness, are used in ladies' hair, but also for wrapping.

Bag of rubber bands
Synthetic rubber
$3\,^7/_8 \times 4\,^7/_8$ in. (10 x 12.5 cm)
Kalbadevi Road, Mumbai, April 2003
Here is a nice assortment of silicone rubber bands in fluorescent colors that should delight
potential customers.

ऑटो रिक्शा ऑटो रिक्शा

वाहन वाहन

साईकल साईकल

टैक्सी टैक्सी

ब्रेक मारना ब्रेक ब्रेक मारना

इन्डिकेटर इन्डिकेटर

गाड़ी गाड़ी

वार्निंग

वार्निंग लाईट वार्निंग लाईट

Transportation — Taxi — Car —

Signal — Brake — Warning

The wildest decorative invention is expressed on Indian modes of transportation. Eschewing any preoccupation with comfort, the owners of motorcycles, bicycles, or motor scooters—like the drivers of trucks, taxis, or auto rickshaws—striving to outdo each other in imagination and daring, transform their vehicles into mobile masterpieces. Their goal is not only decorative: Many of these accessories are designed to give the driver additional protection on the rather deadly roads. Pom-poms of gold and silver thread dangling behind the wheels, little black ragged clogs hanging under the bumpers, saints bedecked with LEDs flashing in the night, and hearts and flowers festooning vehicles constitute as many signs, jujus, and talismans in an attempt to guarantee a long and flourishing life. Private automobiles are, as a whole, less highly adorned. In general, they belong to representatives of the middle class, whose buying power is increasing and whose religious faith is dwindling. To distinguish themselves from working-class drivers, they prefer to abandon the gaudy accessories listed above. Besides, they are disdainful of magic powers.

They are vehicles of an age which it is difficult to define: extremely angular, I could almost say bony, scaringly narrow, reduced to the bone, or rather to the rusty iron. Absolutely tiny: little more roomy than wheelbarrows, with a motor which one starts with a handle in front like in the old films. All painted in vibrant colours, from sky blue to green, from rust to red: and on the front, in flowery letters for anyone who might have doubts, is written PUBLIC CARRIER.

One meets dozens of them in every corner of the street: full of sombre and gentle Indians, of mothers, of children who never cry.

Pier Paolo Pasolini, *The Scent of India*
London: The Olive Press, 1985

Rickshaw — Bicycle

Mudguards
Leatherette, metal, cardboard, plastic
11 x 11 3/4 in. (28 x 30 cm)
Mumbai, Jamshedji Petit Road, Grant Road, April 2003
This style of mudguard, which has appeared relatively recently, adorns an increasing number of taxis, as well as some private automobiles, especially in Mumbai. The designs, featuring fish, pierced hearts, crescent moons, spades, and guns, seem to stare at each other from one wheel to the other. The range of colors (red, black, turquoise, peacock blue, yellow, silver, and gold) hardly ever varies, but their conjunction, often unexpected, is always powerful.

Pair of rearview mirrors
Nickel-plated steel, mirror
3 7/8 x 3 7/8 in. (diameter) (10 x 10 cm)
Mumbai, Jamshedji Petit Road, Grant Road, April 2003
With their twisted shafts, these rearview mirrors seem charged with energy, ready to leap forward for an exciting ride.

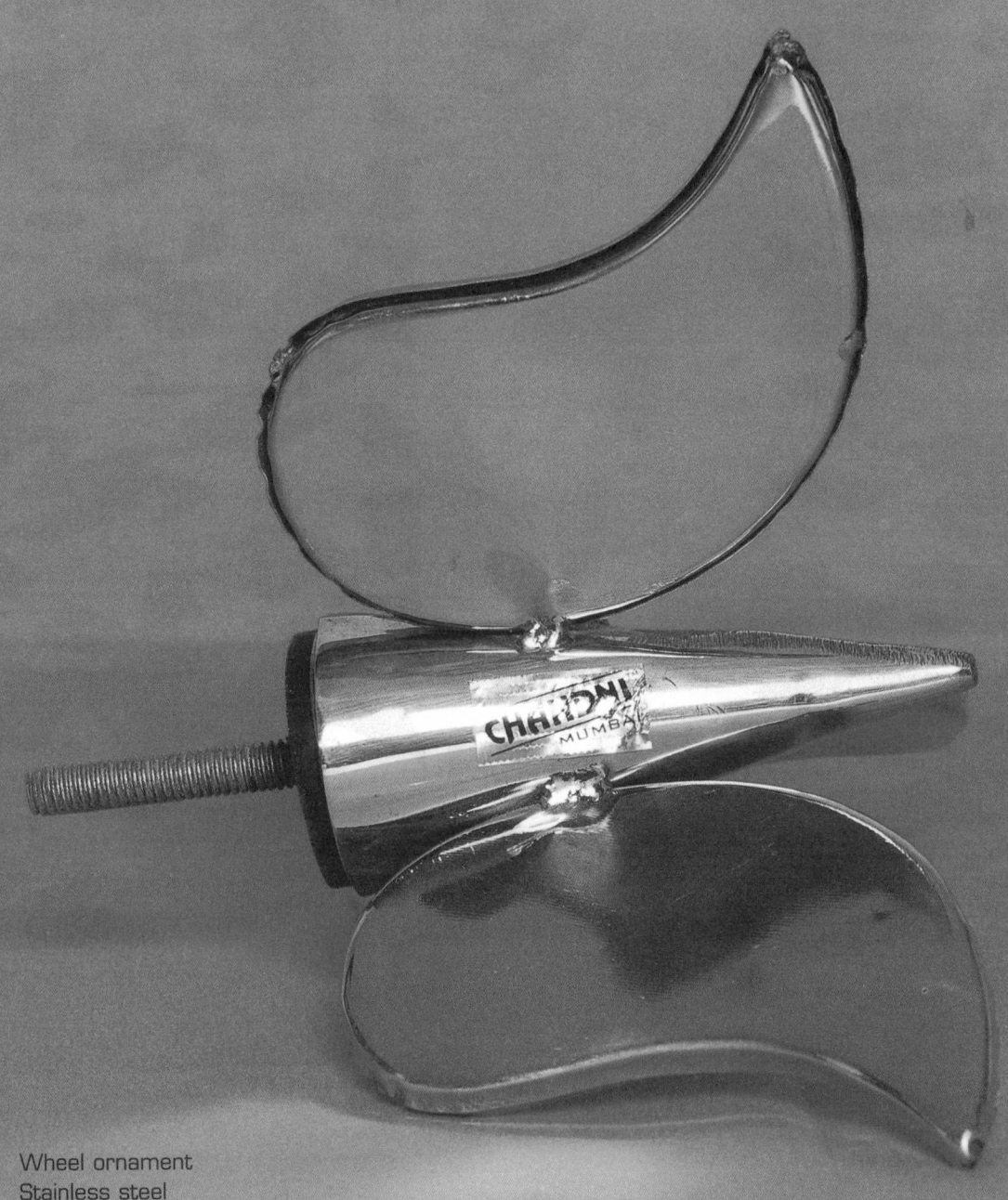

Wheel ornament
Stainless steel
4 1/8 x 6 7/8 in. (10.5 x 17.5 cm)
Mumbai, Jamshedji Petit Road, Grant Road, April 2003
This arrangement of three winged volumes remains an enigma. In fact, given that they will ornament
a rickshaw's wheels, it is certainly odd that the front wheel will be decorated only on one side.

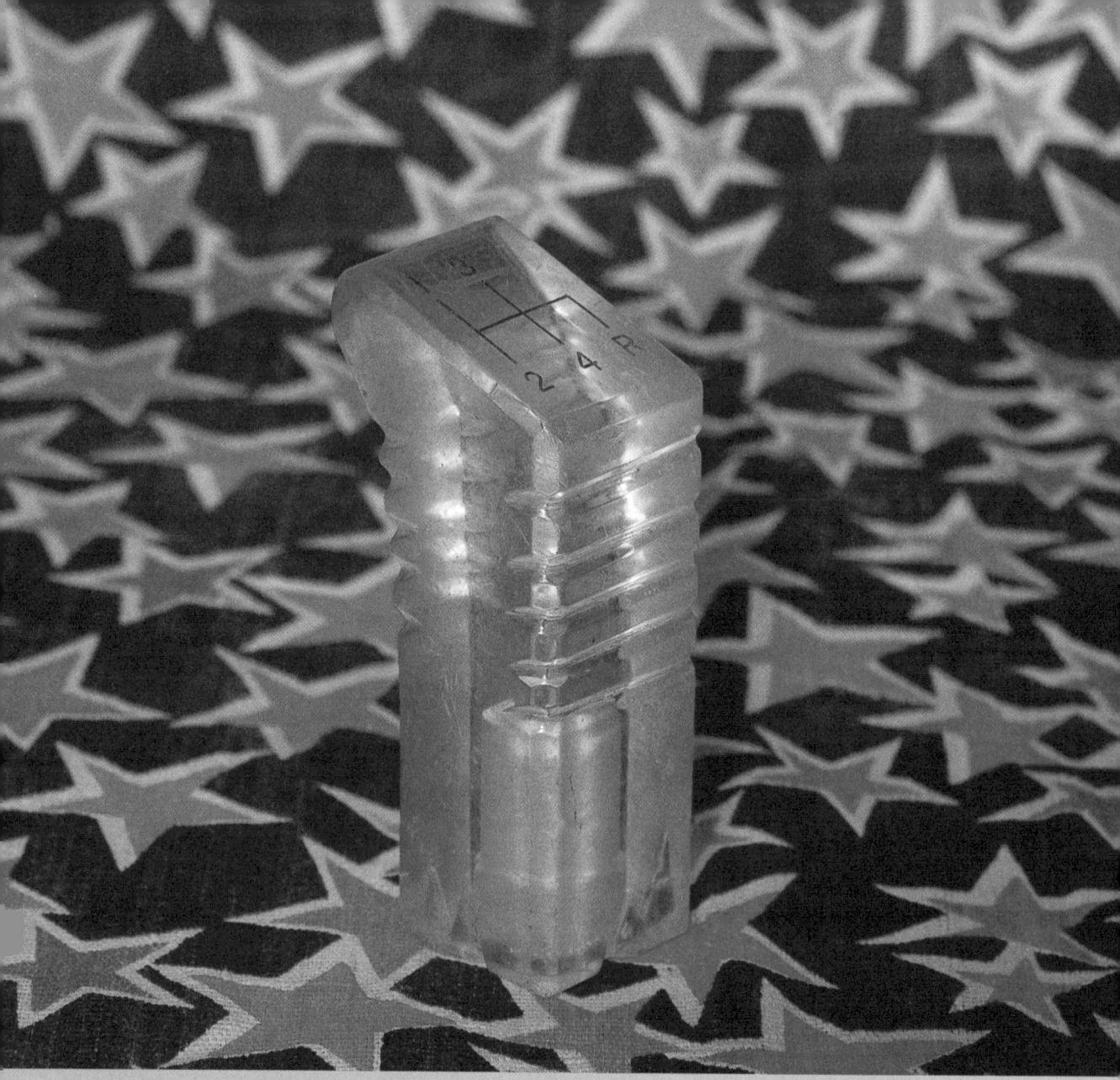

Gearshift knob
Machined acrylic
4 3/8 x 1 3/8 in. (11 x 3.5 cm)
Mumbai, Chor Bazaar, April 2003
The shape of this design is not very practical, and its "big car" look contrasts with the sobriety of the transparent acrylic. In the store in which we found this knob, there was another that seems to have been designed to decorate a stately automobile: A blue neon bulb, fixed within its transparent body, is powered by an electric wire that can be plugged into a car's cigarette lighter. Noticing our enthusiasm for our discovery, the shopkeeper demonstrated it for us. After we had purchased it, however, we discovered, alas, the fatal words "Made in China"! Hence, the second knob isn't depicted here. (A follow-up question: Are commercial ties between India and China, which are increasing, leading to the design of specific models aimed at the presumed taste of the country to which they are exported?)

Gearshift knobs
Anodized aluminum, resin, and plastic
1 5/8–3 x 1 in. (diameter) (4–7.5 x 2.6 cm)
Mumbai, Chor Bazaar, April 2003
The gearshift knobs in this collection, which seems to date from the 1970s and 1980s, are found among many accessories for customizing automobile interiors.

Gearshift knobs
Resin with inlays, threaded
1 3/4 x 1 3/4 in. (4.5 x 4.5 cm)
Mumbai, Chor Bazaar, April 2003
This style exists in many variations.

Brake pedal
Aluminum
4 1/2 x 4 3/4 in. (11.5 x 12 cm)
Mumbai, Chimna Butcher Street, Grant Road, April 2003
Is this clover-leaf brake pedal supposed to bring happiness? In any case, its brand name, Amar, means "eternity" in Hindi. In India, brand names, like given names, are often drawn from religion, nature, or lofty concepts such as truth and precision.

Wheel ornament
Stainless steel
7 1/2 x 5 1/8 in. (diameter) (19 x 13 cm)
Mumbai, Chimna Butcher Street, April 2003
These wheel ornaments live up to their name. The fish in this design, which will doubtless decorate the
wheels of a rickshaw, seem to wriggle. The Anchor company also makes light switches.

Brake light
Colored bulbs, metal, glass, electric wiring
1 $^5/_8$ x 4 $^3/_4$ in. (diameter) (4 x 12 cm)
Mumbai, Chor Bazaar, April 2003
This brake light isn't very bright, but its little colored bulbs light up, blink, and turn whenever the brakes
are applied.

Decorative lights
Plastic, small bulbs, metal, electric wiring
1 5/8–1 3/4 x 1 5/8–3 3/8 in. (4–4.5 x 4–8.5 cm)
Mumbai, Chor Bazaar, April 2003
These three small, luminous objects are intended to decorate a vehicle's dashboard or rear window. The trident (an emblem of Shiva), star, and pinecone don't give off much light, but they seem magical when you see them floating by in the darkness.

Truck turn signals
Colored glass in metal, electric wiring
5 1/2 x 3 1/8 in. (14 x 8 cm)
Mumbai, Chor Bazaar, April 2003
In addition to their nominal function, these turn signals decorate Indian trucks with little colored lights, to the great delight of their drivers, who are crazy about this kind of decoration. The sheet-metal frame into which the glass is recessed is cut out in different shapes: stars, flowers, and even arrows.

Accessory truck lights
Metal, glass, bulbs, electric wiring
1 1/8 x 4 3/8 in. (diameter) (3 x 11 cm)
Mumbai, Chor Bazaar, April 2003
Attached to the side of a truck, these turn signals increase the driver's prestige.

Car radios
Painted metal
1 3/8 x 5 1/2 x 1 3/4 in. (3.5 x 14 x 4.5 cm)
Mumbai, Chor Bazaar, April 2003
These car radios of silk-screened sheet metal are stripped down to the bare essentials, but there is still
a choice between two colors and two slightly different graphic designs!

Self-adhesive "eyes"
Plastic-impregnated adhesive paper
Approx. 1 $\frac{3}{4}$ x 5 $\frac{3}{8}$ in. (4.5 x 13.5 cm)
Mumbai, Chor Bazaar, April 2003
Self-adhesive stickers shaped like eyes are very popular and infinitely varied: metallic, silk screened, line drawn, holographic, fluorescent. No Fear is an American brand name.

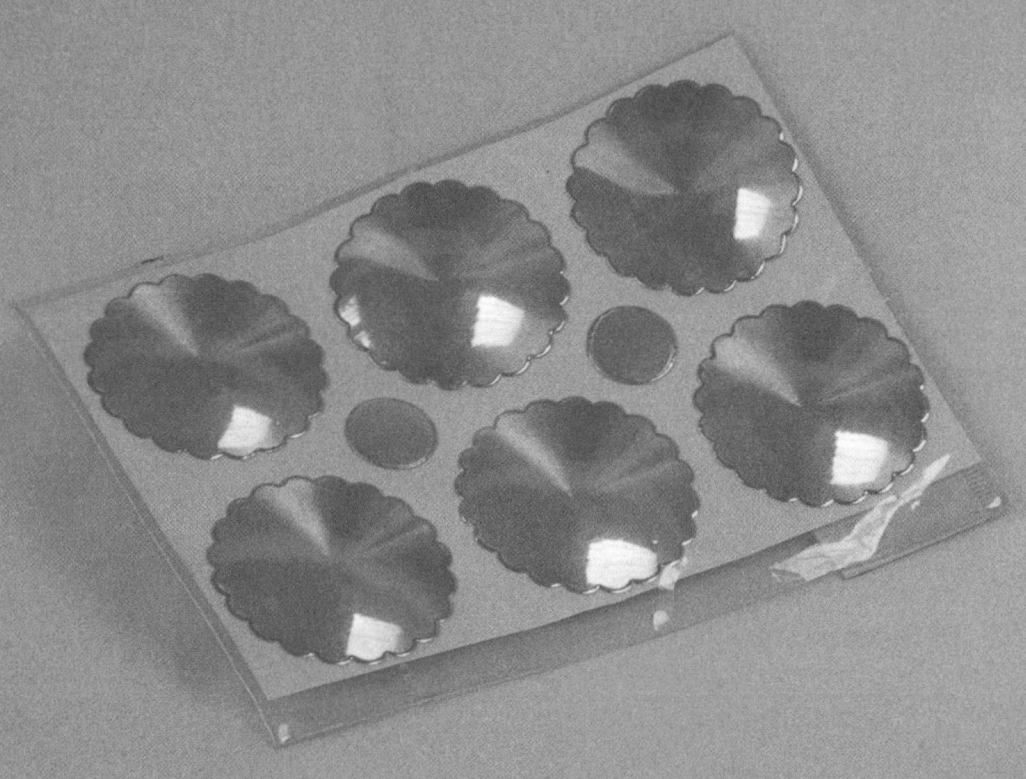

Reflective self-adhesive disks, trimmed with fancy edging
Metallic, plastic-impregnated adhesive paper
$3/8$ x 1 $3/8$ in. (diameter) (0.8 x 3.5 cm)
Mumbai, Chor Bazaar, April 2003
The kinetic effect of these disks, which decorate bicycles and other means of transportation—even trucks—is highly esteemed.

Cow ornament
Metal, leatherette, electric cable
2 7/8 x 1 3/4 x 3 1/4 in. (7.2 x 4.3 x 8.3 cm)
Mysore, February 1998
Is this little cow, whose eyes light up at night, a tribute to the oxen who once drew wagons? In the countryside, tractors are often decorated with a little figurehead in the shape of an ox. Also seen in this image are the reflective stickers, sold in rolls, that decorate bicycles and cars. The long plastic cylinder with a striped yellow design spruces up brake cables, among other things.

Saddle cover
Plastic, foam rubber, plastic piping
10 5/8 x 2 in. (27 x 5 cm)
Mumbai, Kalbadevi Road, April 2003
Because the simple manufacture of bicycle-seat covers is within the reach of almost anyone who wants
to take advantage of the market, infinite variations on this theme exist. This one, in shiny black, is soberly
decorated with white, but the ragged outlines of the drawing betray its homemade origins. Still, the paint
is holding up well.

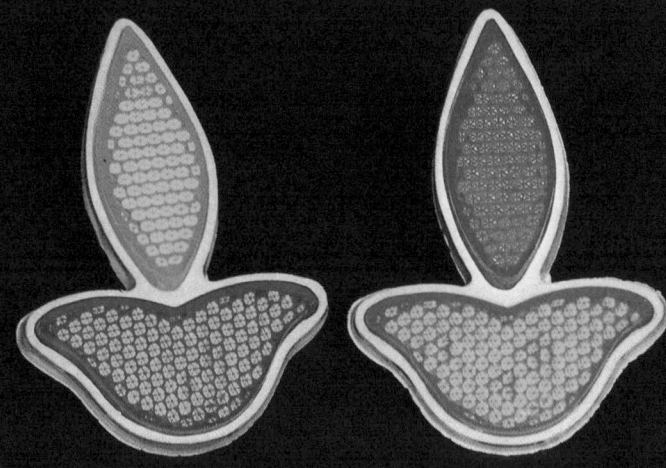

Reflectors
Plastic and metal
2 3/4 x 2 3/4 in. (7 x 7 cm)
Mumbai, Kalbadevi Road, April 2003
This design in the shape of an oil lamp pays a nice tribute to artificial lighting.

Bicycle reflectors
Plastic
2 x 1³/₈ in. (5 x 3.5 cm)
Mumbai, Kalbadevi Road, April 2003
An impressive choice is available to those who want to deck a bicycle out with reflectors. Displays
generally offer a wide range of colors.

Fork brush
Nylon and metal
11 3/4 in. (30 cm)
Mumbai, Kalbadevi Road, April 2003
This sweep clips to the center of the bicycle wheel and turns as the rider pedals, giving maximum effect with a minimum of expense.

Bicycle-spoke balls
Injection-molded plastic
3/4 in. (diameter) (2 cm)
Mumbai, Kalbadevi Road, April 2003
These little multicolored items clip to the wheels and tinkle joyously as they slide along the spokes when the wheel turns.

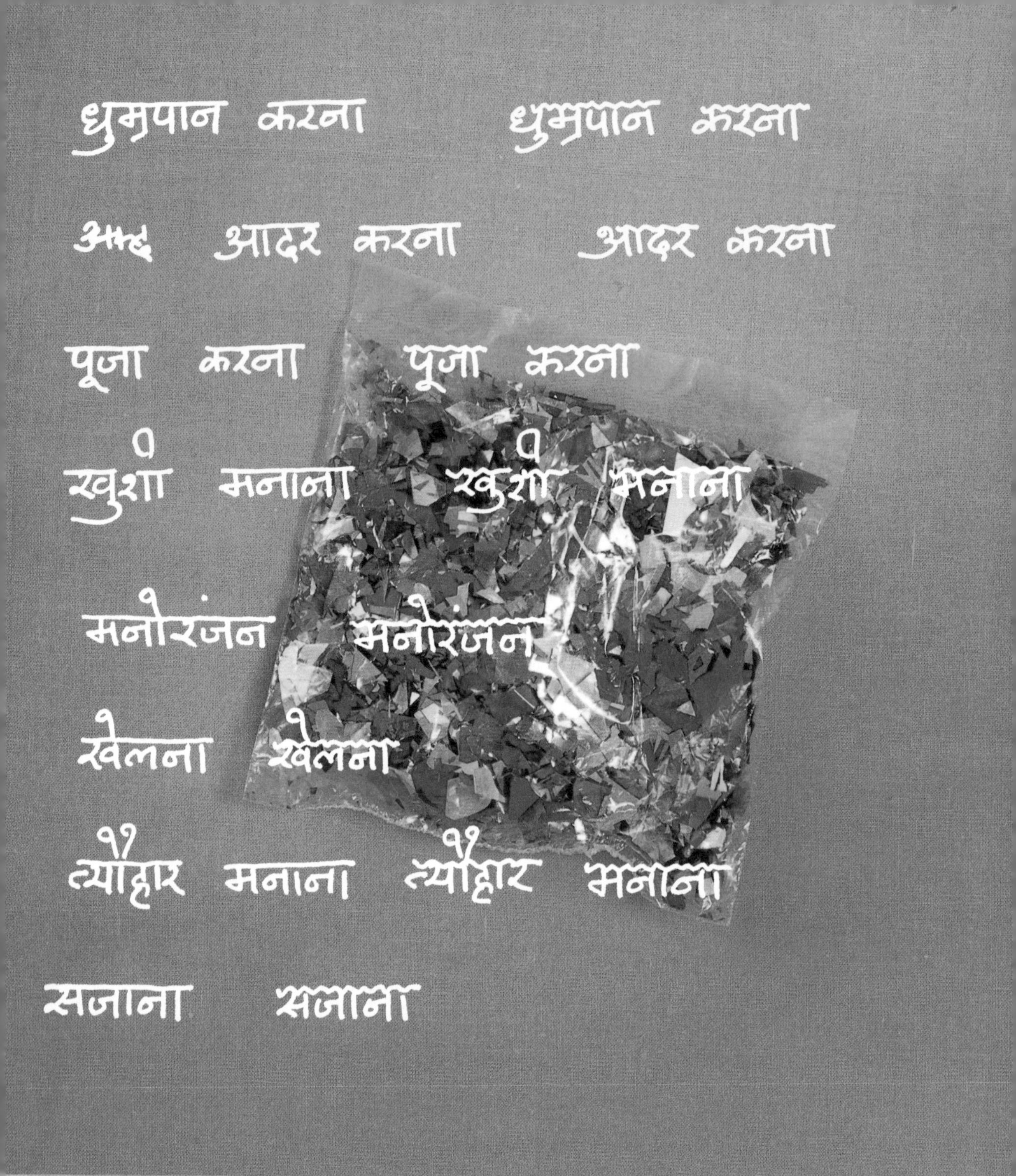

धुम्रपान करना   धुभ्रपान करना

अन्ह आदर करना   आदर करना

पूजा करना   पूजा करना

खुशी मनाना   खुशी मनाना

मनोरंजन   मनोरंजन

खेलना   खेलना

त्यौहार मनाना   त्यौहार मनाना

सजाना   सजाना

Toast — Honor — Enjoy — Celebrate —

Learn — Copy — Jingle — Watch

Ephemeral decorations in India have a magical ability to last. Throughout the year, they hang, decorate, adorn, sparkle, illuminate. In houses, on rickshaws, in the streets, on doors in shantytowns, or in trees, garlands, banners, wreaths, and strings of fresh or paper flowers are combined with perilous electrical installations, taking up residence until they are replaced for the next holiday. Indian holidays, lay or religious, are numerous, and each has its own ritual. For Holi, the Feast of Colors, which marks the arrival of spring, young people—especially boys—carry special pumps and spray passersby with colored pigments. The most violent crimsons, pinks, saffron yellows, and turquoise blues, and sometimes powdered silver, settle in long, indelible streams on the clothing and in the hair of anyone who dares to go outside unprotected. The rise of urban institutions, however, is diminishing these ritual excesses, and the new outbursts are more violent. For Divali, lanterns and garlands are hung, candles are lit, and firecrackers and fireworks are set off. At Christmas, balls of artificial snow are displayed. Marriages, of course, are an occasion for demonstrations of decorative splendor, such as rose-petal bombs that explode in the air, scattering petals to fall slowly on the wedding guests. Parties and decorations, colors and nuances, frills and glamour are an integral part of the everyday routine.

It was late when Amma found it. The house shone with the flames of the oil lamps she had set out along the terrace wall. . . . At sunset she had performed her ritual, then lit the lamps. . . . The sky, which exploded with firecrackers and rockets, was brilliant with gold and silver.

Bulbul Sharma, *The Anger of Aubergines: Stories of Women and Food*
New Delhi: Kali for Women, 1997

Play — Decorate — Smoke — Enjoy

Bidis
Anywhere in the street
Tobacco leaf and paper
2 3/8–3 7/8 in. (6–10 cm)
"Both of them will live at my house and they'll sleep in my bed," he thought, taking a long drag of his bidi
. . . Nath very carefully slipped the half-smoked bidi behind his ear and tackled the sloping path. . . . He
pulled out his bidi and lit up again. The taste of tobacco mingled with that of mushrooms as he stood there
and exhaled clouds of smoke, watching the bluish trail disappear through the branches."

Bulbul Sharma, *The Anger of Aubergines: Stories of Women and Food*
New Delhi: Kali for Women, 1997

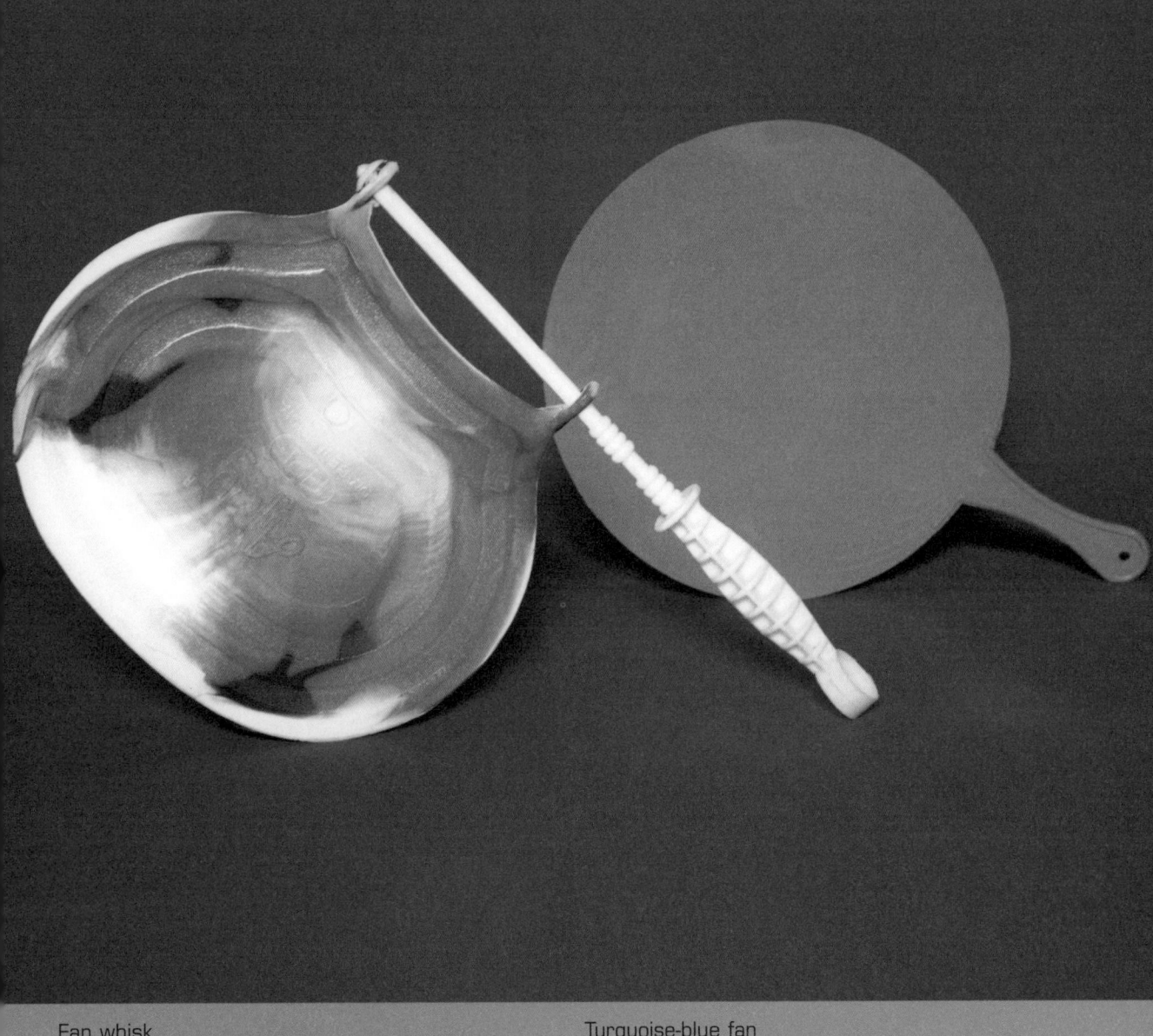

Fan whisk
Plastic
10 5/8 x 6 1/4 in. (27 x 16 cm)
Jodhpur, February 2001
This fan, which swings on its axis with the slightest
effort, is unusual in that it sends air in every
direction, cooling anyone in the area. Peddlers
who cook and sell snacks in the street often use
these to fan the embers and chase flies away.

Turquoise-blue fan
Plastic
10 5/8 x 7 5/8 in. (diameter) (27 x 19.5 cm)
Jodhpur, February 2001

Hanging decorations
Fluorescent paper
15 3/4 x 1 5/8 in. (diameter) (40 x 4 cm)
Mumbai, Null Bazaar, April 2003
Fitted with a fluorescent frill, these hangings are used for decoration throughout the year. They come in a small package and, thanks to an ingenious drawstring system, unfold as they are hung.

Pink garlands
Plastic-impregnated paper
7 7/8 ft (2.4 m)
Mumbai, Crawford Market, April 2003
Simple decorations within the reach of almost every pocketbook, these garlands are hung out for
traditional holidays, but also on birthdays and at Christmas. They usually remain until they are
replaced by others for a future occasion.

String of flags
Paper and plastic
Varying dimensions
Mumbai, Null Bazaar, April 2003
For holidays, religious or otherwise, at the least excuse, these strings of flags are hung inside houses, in courtyards, in the streets, and along the path of marriage processions. Plastic obviously stands up to the elements better than paper, which it has largely replaced. Very light and rather fragile, these inexpensive decorations are hugely popular.

Garland
Multicolored synthetic velvet
Variable length x $3/8$ in. (diameter) (1 cm)
Mumbai, Null Bazaar, April 2003
These garlands are hung from statues of gods and on portraits of those to be honored, as well as from roofs of rickshaws, from rearview mirrors, or any other place to be protected and enlivened.

Garland
Metalic plastic
86 x $3/4$ in. (diameter) (220 x 2 cm)
Mumbai, Null Bazaar, April 2003

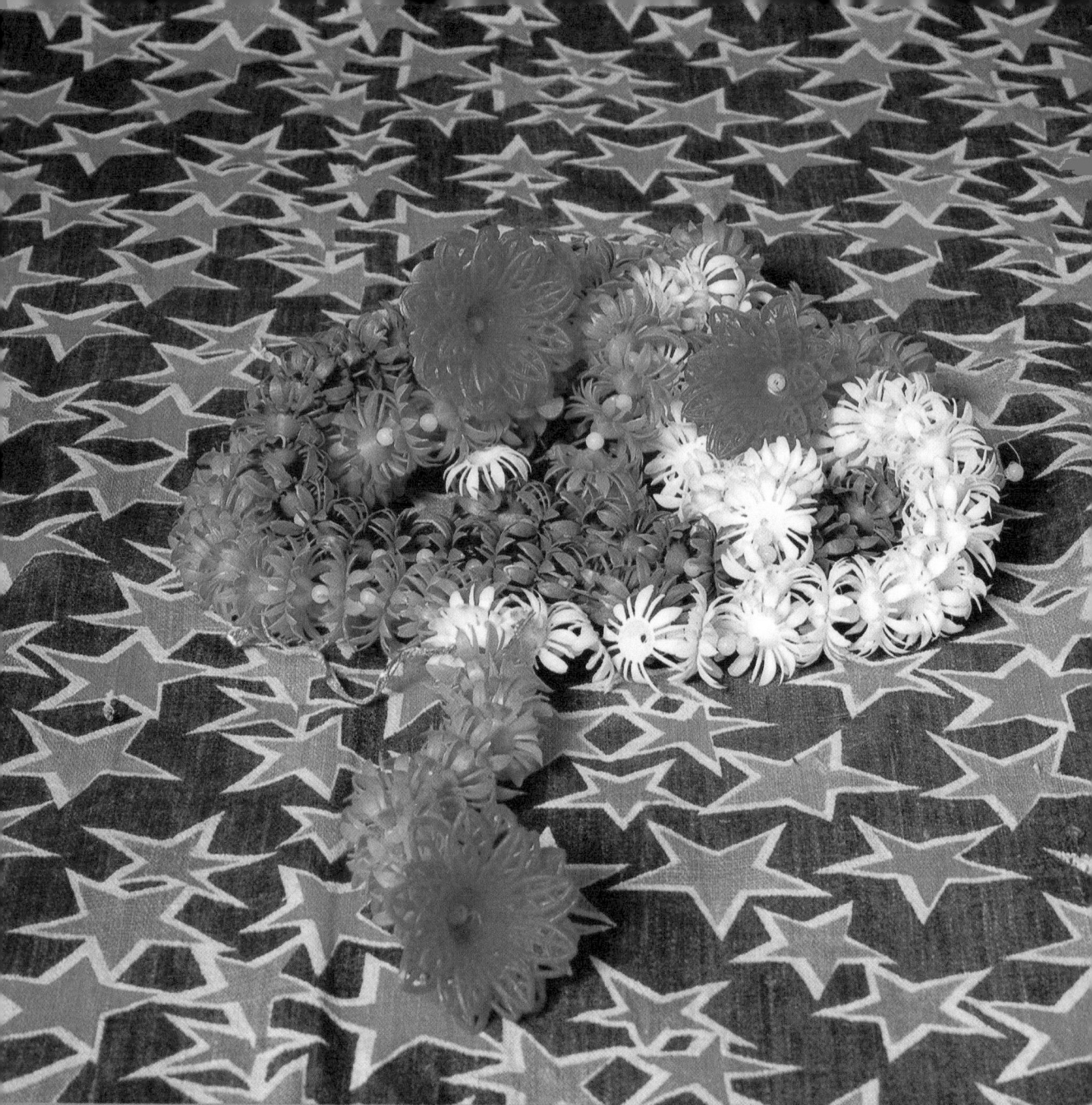

Garland
Red, white, orange, and green plastic
3 1/4 ft x 3/4 in. (diameter) (1 m x 2 cm)
Mumbai, Null Bazaar, April 2003
These garlands are found in infinite versions. Very common, they wear India's national colors: saffron, white, and green. Their pieces are reminiscent of the most popular flowers in the country: jasmine and little carnations. Made like a necklace with a pendant, they adorn portraits, photographs, and hand-tinted drawings of gods, gurus, and ancestors that decorate the most important rooms of apartments and shops. Fresh flowers are more often used in temples and to decorate the living to honor them.

Bouquet
Colored paper and iron wire
Life-size
Mumbai, Null Bazaar, April 2003
This fragile bouquet, still vivid but already a little faded (the paper bleaches very quickly), is one of the many decorations inexpensive enough to be hung up at will.

Anil Atom Bomb — Fireworks
Powder, string, cardboard
3 x ³/4 in. (diameter) (7.5 x 2 cm)
Jaipur, Chandpole Bazaar, February 2001

These fireworks come from Sivakasi, a city in the state of Tamil Nadu that produces almost 80 percent of the fireworks and matches made in India. As the cover indicates, they're particularly noisy: The string

that wraps the powder compresses it to make the resulting explosion especially loud. Note the label: In firecrackers, we see reflected India's joy in finally possessing the atomic bomb. A popular expression echoes the pride Indians feel in belonging to the international nuclear-weapons club: When you say of someone that he or she "made a *pokhran!*" (nuclear bomb), that means that the person hit the jackpot.

"National Integration" disposable napkins, Jackson brand
Absorbent paper and cardboard
6 3/4 x 6 3/4 x 3 1/8 in. (17 x 17 x 8 cm)
Mumbai, Royal Yacht Club, April 2003

Cups
Injection-molded plastic
3 7/8 x 2 1/2 in. (diameter) (9.7 x 6.5 cm)
Mumbai, Null Bazaar, February 1999

In this country, a melting pot of ethnicity, culture, and religion, the box holding these napkins preaches harmony among all. Jackson brand packaging celebrates national unity and communicates a good-natured message, echoing the campaign the government conducts regularly to promote civic harmony and democratic principles. Because many Indians are illiterate, a simple illustration reinforces the message, and "National Integration" paper napkins convey it in an attempt to increase Jackson's market share—and the brand likely receives a government subsidy, too. These practices explain why civic messages are found in the most unexpected places. As for the assortment of plastic cups, they drew our eye with their gentle colors: yellows, greens, and blues.

Paper dishes
Leaves, wrapping paper, plastic-covered cardboard
1 5/8–7 1/8 in. (diameter) (4–18 cm)
Mumbai, Null Bazaar, April 2003
These little paper plates of various sizes have long been popular in India. Originally made of dried and pressed banana leaves, they are used to serve the many snacks offered in the streets, as well as at feasts and marriages. Today, throwaway materials of all kinds, such as paper of varying quality or cardboard, plastic coated or not, are used in their manufacture. The dishes pictured, made from boxes in which products as diverse as baby food, cooking utensils, tissues, or saris were packaged, have a thick plastic covering, and reveal a marked taste for a brightly colored and vigorous graphic style.

Cassette player
Sheet metal, silk-screened decoration, flashing LEDs
5 1/8 x 9 x 6 1/4 in. (13 x 23 x 16 cm)
Mumbai, Chor Bazaar, February 1999
Cassette players like this one, once very common, were assembled in numerous small workshops and highly customized. Their prestige is proportional to the number of LEDs that begin to flash as soon as a tape is played. (The complexity of the decoration is supposed to reflect their technological sophistication.) They may be thought of as a popular form of applied art, but, today, they have disappeared from the shelves to make way for new black streamlined models—Japanese, or imitations thereof.

Flowerpots (fireworks)
Powder, string, cardboard
3 3/8 x 1 5/8 in. (diameter) (8.5 x 4 cm)
Jaipur, Chandpole Bazaar, February 2001
These conical fireworks, which produce fountains of light, are used mostly at the time of Divali. Sometimes they malfunction, causing accidents the newspapers report the morning after the feasts. They are mostly made in Sivakasi. A movie star's portrait decorates the box; in India, it is not necessary to pay celebrities for the right to use their likeness, so portraits of Bollywood actors and actresses show up in the oddest places.

Indians, even those faced with great difficulties, are on the whole tender and attentive toward their children. Residences are often shared among all the members of the family, and uncles, aunts, brothers-in-law, sisters-in-law, or grandparents take turns caring for the young. This vigilance extends to all children of an apartment building or a city block in cities, and in the countryside to all the village children. Government campaigns to limit births, broadcast throughout the country over the last few decades, have reduced the birth rate, making babies seem even more precious.

The most recent generation of children is thus rather spoiled, as the marketing of an increased number of objects designed for their amusement reveals. There is a definite taste for miniaturized adult things, such as tea sets, furniture, motorcycles, and rickshaws, tools for learning the gestures and roles of everyday life. For little girls, there are plates, dishes, mixers, pails, basins, and stoves, and little boys enjoy kites (still very popular), piggy banks, and little automobiles.

Wheeled toys
Plastic
2–2 3/4 x 2 3/4–4 3/4 in. (5–7 x 7–12 cm)
Jaipur, Sanjay Bazaar, October 2003
These little wheeled toys, of a rather dubious quality, are quite popular, and reflect all the figures of daily Indian life: elephants, parrots, scooters, rickshaws, swans, peacocks, and so on.

Alphabet
Wood
15 ³/₄ x 8 ⁷/₈ in. (40 x 22.5 cm)
Delhi, Khan Market, October 2003
This big wooden puzzle board has an unavoidable educational motive.

Rattles
Tin
5 3/8 x 2 1/2 in. (diameter) (13.5 x 6.5 cm)
4 1/4 x 1 1/8 in. (diameter) (11 x 3 cm)
Jaipur, Tholia Bazaar, February 1999
The jingling rattle is one of those things, like padlocks, one is almost certain to see on almost any shelf in
a dry-goods store in India. Child-care equipment there is rather modest, but the rattle seems indispensable.
These tin bells, joined in the shape of a dumbbell, or formed like a tin drum and decorated with green
and pink designs, are being supplanted by plastic ones.

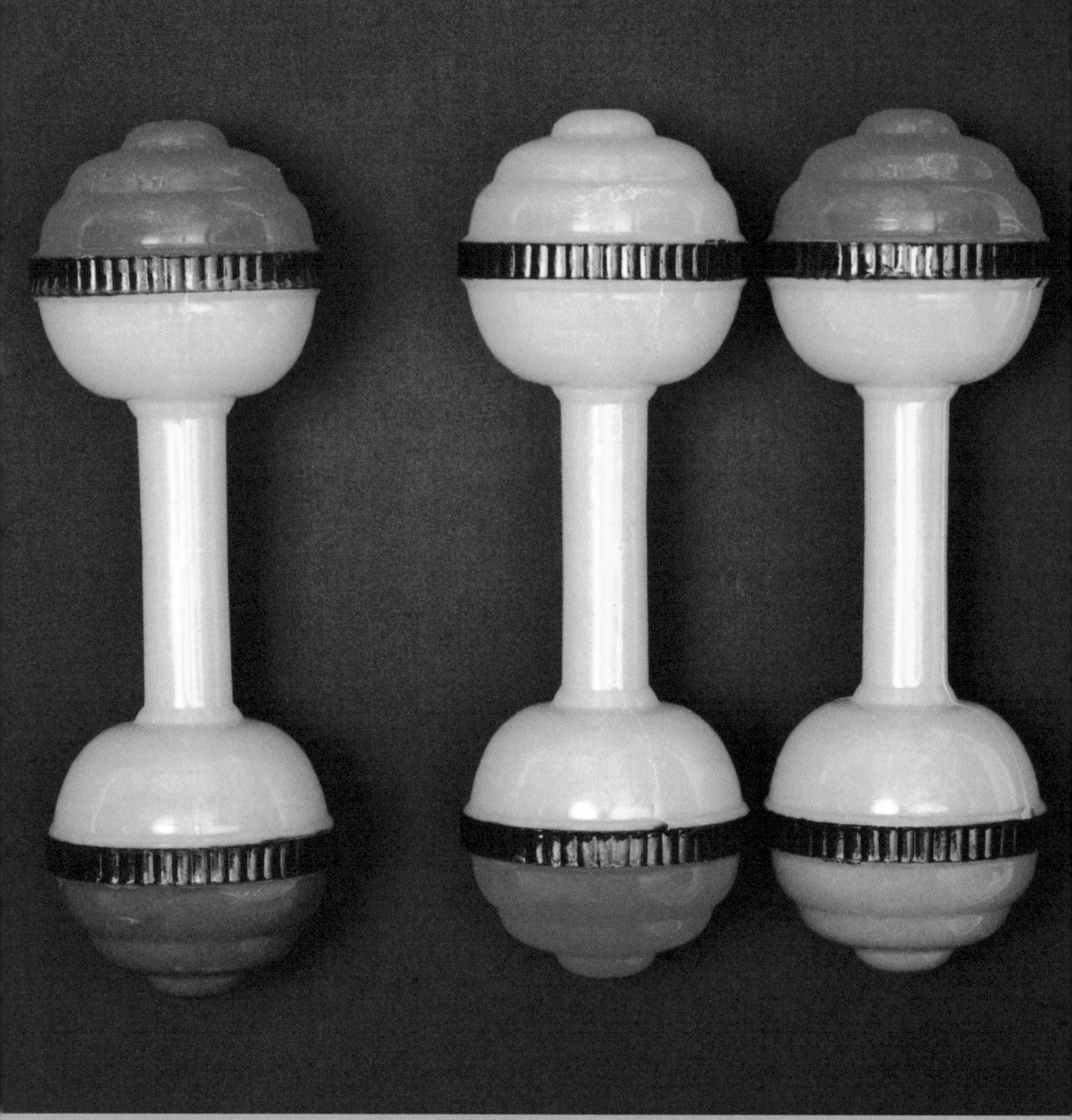

Rattle
Tricolored plastic
5 1/2 x 2 in. (diameter) (14 x 5 cm)
Mumbai, Mangaldas Road, April 2003
In the world of toys, as in many other markets, metal is slowly giving way to plastic. This recent version
is shaped like a dumbbell.

Hammer rattle
5 7/8 x 3 1/2 in. (15 x 9 cm)
Plastic
Mumbai, Mangaldas Road, April 2003

Rattle
6 1/8 x 2 in. (diameter) (15.5 x 5 cm)
Plastic
Mumbai, Mangaldas Road, April 2003

It's too bad you can't hear the sound these rattles make; they're rather sweet and crystalline, or slightly harsh.

Kite reels and string
Plastic and nylon
8 1/4 x 2 1/2 in. (diameter) (21 x 6.5 cm)
Jaipur, Bara Bazaar, February 2002

Kite flying is a popular sport, and several people often play competitively at once: The kite string may be covered with an abrasive so it will cut an adversary's string. (Trees and electrical wires are often hung with defeated kites that have come to rest there, their tissue paper bleached by the sun.) Powdered glass is applied by hand to the string over an impressive length—between about 50 and 65 feet (15 and 20 meters)—as it is stretched between two trees or two people: When a kite festival occurs, the streets are filled with makeshift workshops where this process is performed. An image of Govinda, a Bollywood cult actor from the 1990s, affixed to the reel marks the popular and good-natured character of this game.

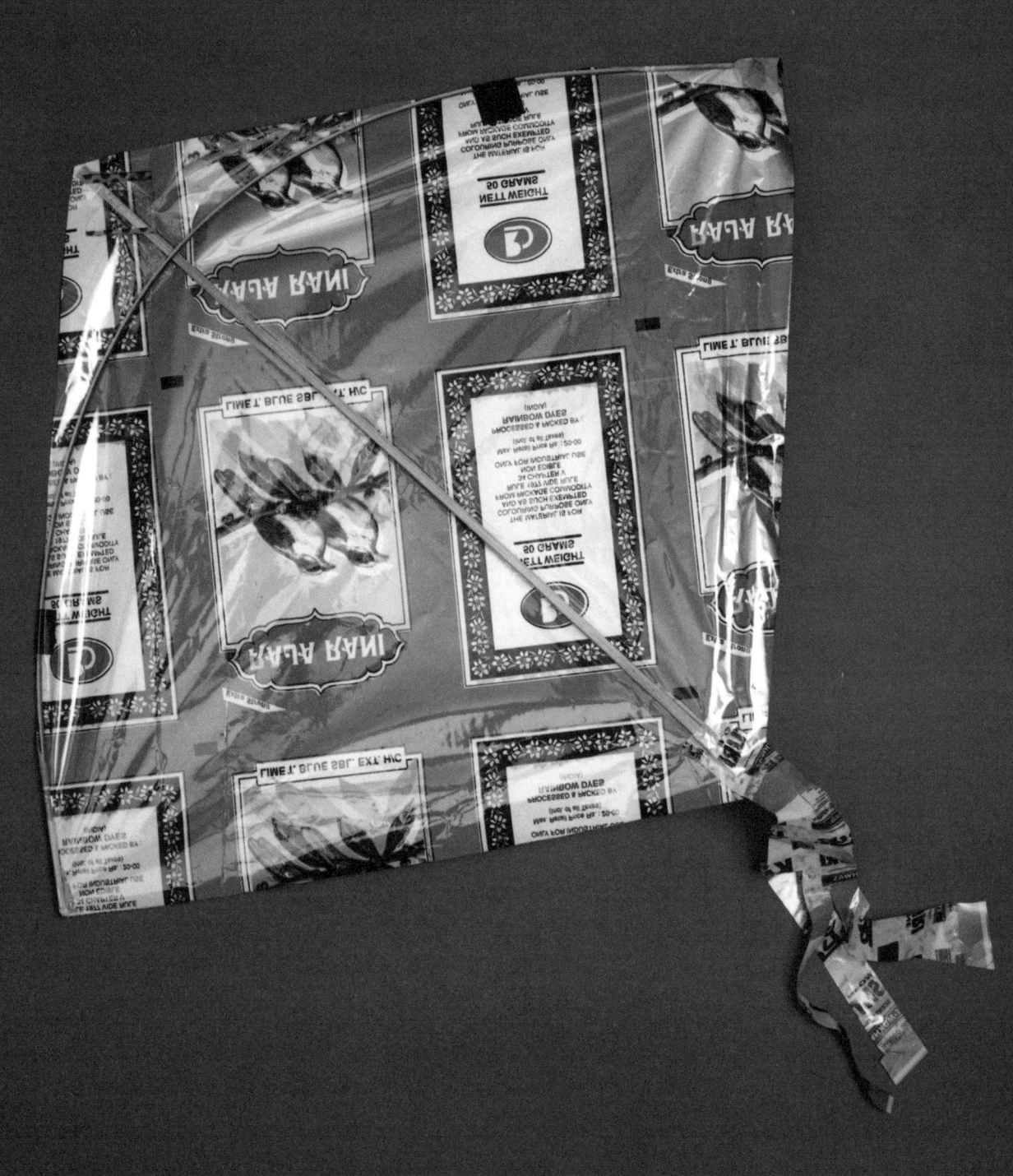

Kite
Plastic film and paper
11 x 11 3/8 in. (28 x 29 cm)
Mumbai, April 2003
The paper of traditional kites is giving way to plastic, which obviously stands up better to rain, but whose shreds disappear more slowly as they hang from trees.

Piggy banks
Printed sheet metal
4 x 3 $\frac{1}{8}$ in. (diameter) (10.2 x 8 cm)
Mumbai, Null Bazaar, April 2003

Packaging materials, especially tin cans, are often recycled and put to new uses. Here, with new lids soldered on, they are turned into piggy banks.

Toy dishes
Metal and plastic
1 1/8–2 3/4 in. (3.5–7 cm) (height and diameter)
Jaipur, Nehru Market, January 1998; Mumbai, Kalbadevi Road, April 2003;
Jaipur, Sanjay Market, October 2003
A touching attention to realism informs these toy dishes: Playthings are serious business, and children
are demanding clients. These are exact reproductions, admirably miniaturized, of common utensils; little
by little plastic is replacing painted metal. Adults, not impervious to the charms of these little replicas,
are often drawn to them, and display them at home as knickknacks.

Toy mixers
Plastic
2 3/4–4 1/2 x 2 3/8–3 in. (7–11.5 x 6–7.5 cm)
Jaipur, February 1999; Mumbai, Kalbadevi Road, April 2003; Jaipur, Sanjay Bazaar, October 2003
In order to avoid any confusion with the famous brand name Sumeet (see page 131), the *m* on the label has been changed to an *n*.

Toy dish drainer
Stainless steel and cardboard
$10^1/4$ x $7^7/8$ in. (26 x 20 cm)
Mumbai, Kalbadevi Road, April 2003
Stainless-steel dish drainers, found hanging from the wall above the sink in most Indian kitchens,
are used as much for storing as for drying dishes. Miniature versions such as this one are invariably
included in sets of toy dishes, which may be purchased, among other places, in stores that sell real ones.

Toy wardrobe
Metal
6 1/4 x 3 1/2 x 2 in. (16 x 9 x 5 cm)
Mumbai, Kalbadevi Road, April 2003
Deriving directly from the bureaucratic world brought to India by the British, the sheet-metal wardrobe, clothed in official-looking prestige, has rapidly conquered the Indian household, in which—except for chests, and niches hollowed into the walls—such furniture did not heretofore exist. In the 1990s, the addition of a large mirror to one of the doors definitively established the wardrobe; practical and secure, it became very popular. Many small workshops produce this design with variations, such as a delicate little flower ground into the mirror (absent from this miniaturized version). The most famous wardrobe manufacturer is Godrej, which also makes hair dye and many other unrelated products.

Toy cook stove
Metal and plastic
3 7/8 x 2 in. (diameter) (10 x 5 cm)
Jaipur, Sanjay Bazaar, October 2003
The manufacturer of this object, in a quest for realism, didn't skimp on the number of parts. Labor is inexpensive, and it doesn't matter much if there are five pieces to be assembled: The result is successful, and the toy is a faithful reproduction of the real thing.

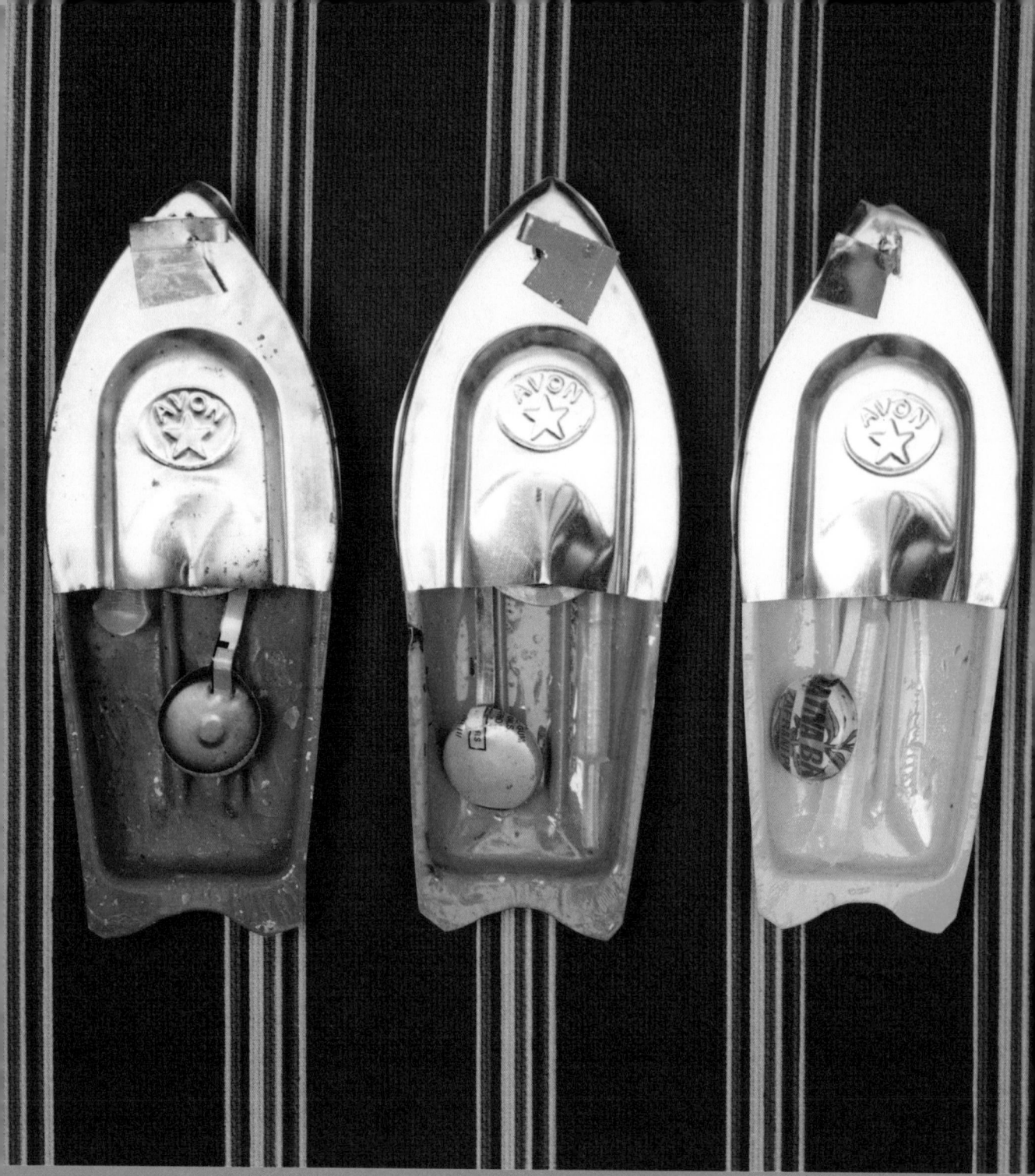

Toy boats
Painted metal
5 1/2 x 2 1/8 in. (14 x 5.5 cm)
Mumbai, Colaba, April 2003

These little boats, made from recycled sheet metal and decorated with a few strokes of the brush, are of prodigious ingenuity: When the wick is lit, they putt-putt across the water.

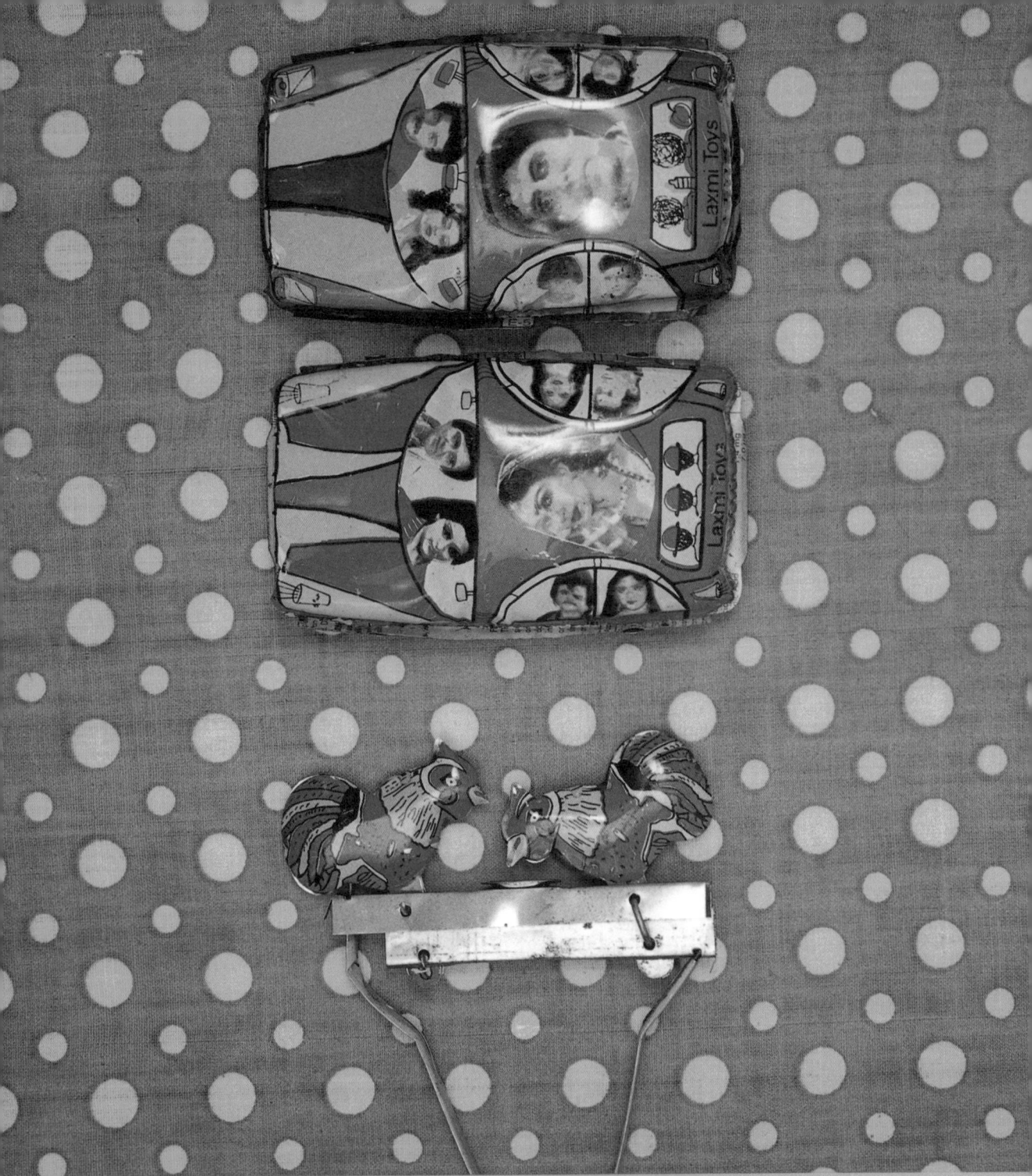

Toy cars and rattle
Printed tin
3 7/8 x 2 3/8 in. (10 x 6 cm)
Jaipur, Sanjay Bazaar, October 2003
This rattle incorporates the classic motif of two hens pecking at an imaginary plate of grain.

सीखना	सीखना
रसोई	रसोई
तलना	तलना
काटना	काटना
घिसना	घिसना
छिड़कना	छिड़कना
परोसना	परोसना
साचा	साचा
पकाना	पकाना
छानना	छानना
डालना	डालना

(प्लास्टिक की) खुर्पी

मिठाई का डिब्बा मिठाई का डिब्बा

Fry — Chop — Grate —

Cook — Filter — Pour

Indian cuisine is considered one of the most sophisticated in the world. Following the principles of Ayurvedic medicine, six flavors—sweet, sour, bitter, salty, astringent, and spicy—are divided into categories associated with earth, water, and fire. Each one of these three elements acts differently on health, mood, and character. Indian cuisine, by infinitely combining the ingredients, blends them. Food preparation, still the business of women, is labor intensive. In traditional households, spices are ground by hand every morning, and a genuine Indian meal consists of many dishes. Depending on religion and region, tastes, habits, and prohibitions vary noticeably, but the national unity of cuisine is ensured throughout the country by the sophisticated and generous use of spices.

Quickly I moved away and began to concentrate on the task at hand. I took a little ceramic bowl, peeled some garlic into it, and threw in a little turmeric and some chili. These I crushed together, gritting my teeth as the smell of their melding came to me. . . .

I put spices into the pot, stirred quickly, and put the lid on. "Can you give me some yoghurt?" I asked without looking at him. "And some sugar." He handed both to me silently. I mixed in the yoghurt. Slowly the bitter acrimony in the pot subsided. I turned the fire down low. . . .

He moved to the stove. "Shall I taste it?"

I nodded. He took a spoon and dipped it into the pot. As he tasted, he stared at me intently. Then his face suddenly relaxed as pleasure filled it.

Radhika Jha, *Smell*
New York: Soho, 2001

Serve — Sprinkle — Unmold

Red-and-white-striped pot
Plastic
9 $^4/_5$ x 9 $^4/_5$ in. (diameter) (25 x 25 cm)
Jaipur, Sanjay Bazaar, October 2003
This pot has many attractions: It is at once iridescent, striped with brilliant red, and ornamented with a delicate frieze of flowers in bas-relief. It is designed to be held by the neck.

Water pots
Plastic
Jaipur, Sanjay Bazaar, October 2003
7 $^1/_8$–8 $^5/_8$ x 5 $^7/_8$–7 $^7/_8$ in. (diameter) (18–22 x 15–20 cm)
Despite an innovative material and a color that is exhausting, these water jugs remain faithful to the
eternal shape of the traditional pot, which women carry on their heads when they return from the well.

Cook stoves
Painted steel
Variable dimensions
Mumbai, Chor Bazaar, April 2003
These kerosene-burning cook stoves, also known by the generic term *coolha* (place for cooking), are of different sizes and colored like cockatoos. The scarlet, fuchsia, and emerald-green ones stand out. On models for individual use, the fuel tank is directly beneath the burner, while the reservoirs for family-size models that can hold big pots are located on the side. Middle-class families hardly ever use such stoves, but they still keep one as a backup in case of gas shortages. The varieties of metal stands, square or round, that define the stove illustrate the significant notion of good conservation of materials.

Strainers
Aluminum, tin, stainless steel, metal or plastic mesh
7 5/8–8 5/8 x 2 7/8–3 3/8 in. (19.5–22 x 7.2–8.7 cm) (diameter)
Tonk, February 1999; Jaipur, Nehru Bazaar, February 2001; Delhi, March 2001
Chai is prepared by boiling sugar, tea, and spices in milk, which is then filtered just before it is served. An infinite quantity of styles of *chai* strainers exist throughout the land, where, on every street corner and in every home, at every moment, everyone is drinking it. The strainers filter out the grains of cardamom and ginger, as well as tea leaves and other ingredients, so they don't float in the cup or glass. These objects are created with the greatest diversity of manufacture, from handcrafting to mass production. From the simple cotton cloth, originally white, through which the beverage is strained to the artistically perforated stainless steel—including one made of pink nylon held in a strip of tin and made right on the sidewalk and another formed from solid sterling silver—there is one for every taste and, especially, every pocketbook.

ush
sted plastic and nylon bristles
⁷/8 in. (13 cm)
hi, Chandni Chowk, February 2001
s brush, although it may serve other needs, is primarily used to brush foods such as cakes of bread
h ghee, a clarified butter often used in cooking.

Mixer
Plastic and metal
15 x 12 $^5/_8$ x 6 $^1/_4$ in. (38 x 32 x 16 cm)
Mumbai, Kansara Chawl, February 1999
This is the archetypal Indian mixer, with virtues unknown today in the West. The most pleasant of these is the change in pitch when the operator switches from one speed to another: The sound of the motor drops, then races off once more. That's why we call this Sumeet model the Formula 1 of mixers. Its sturdiness is legendary, as we've been able to confirm for many years. There is no spice or food that can resist the many accessories the Sumeet proudly supports.

Trays
Painted wood
Wood and laminate
2 1/2 x 14 5/8 x 9 5/8 in. (6.5 x 37 x 24.5 cm)
Mumbai, Zaveri Bazaar, April 2003

Trays
Metal and plastic
3 1/8 x 11 x 7 1/2 in. (8 x 28 x 19 cm)
Mumbai, Null Bazaar, April 2003

Traditionally, there is no work surface, properly speaking, in Indian kitchens: Women squat on the ground and work on a small area kept scrupulously clean. On these little low tables, for example, they knead bread and grind spices. The tables also hold the necessities for prayer: incense, sandalwood powder, and so on.

Pressure cooker
Aluminum and plastic
$4^{3}/_{8} \times 5^{1}/_{2}$ in. (diameter) (11 x 14 cm); approx. 1 qt (1 l) capacity
Mumbai, Null Bazaar, April 2003
Saucepans and other cooking pots range in size from the minuscule to the gigantic, and this pressure cooker is the smallest one we could find. Its little-known brand name would better suit a specimen of more imposing dimensions.

Stove lighter
Stainless steel
$5/8$ x $6 1/2$ in. (1.5 x 16.5 cm)
Delhi, Lajpat Nagar, January 2002
For those who can afford it, this gadget handily replaces the family's big box of matches. With a simple press of the button, the flame appears. Although the flint wears very slowly, a little box of spares comes in the package; there are enough to last a whole lifetime, or even several.

Baking dishes
Hammered aluminum
4 7/8–5 7/8 x 1 3/4–2 3/4 in. (12.5–15 x 4.5–7 cm)
Mumbai, Null Bazaar, April 2003
These casserole dishes come in all sizes and many variations. The most prestigious are tin-plated copper; stainless steel is a little cheaper, and aluminum represents an even lower quality. They may be found with both flat and round bottoms, as well as in metal of varying thicknesses.

Knife
Stainless steel
8 1/4 x 3/4 in. (21 x 2 cm)
Varanasi, February 1997

The handle of this knife is a band of stainless steel folded back on itself and welded to the blade (which can be sharpened). This ingenious design allows for a hollow handle without the necessity of stamping equipment.

Knives
Steel, bamboo, wood, plastic
4 ⁷/₈ x 9 in. (12.5 x 23 cm)
Mumbai, Null Bazaar, April 2003
These knives, which serve as multipurpose tools, are made quite crudely, without tooling, in shantytowns
and villages. Often, the blades come from used and recycled saws.

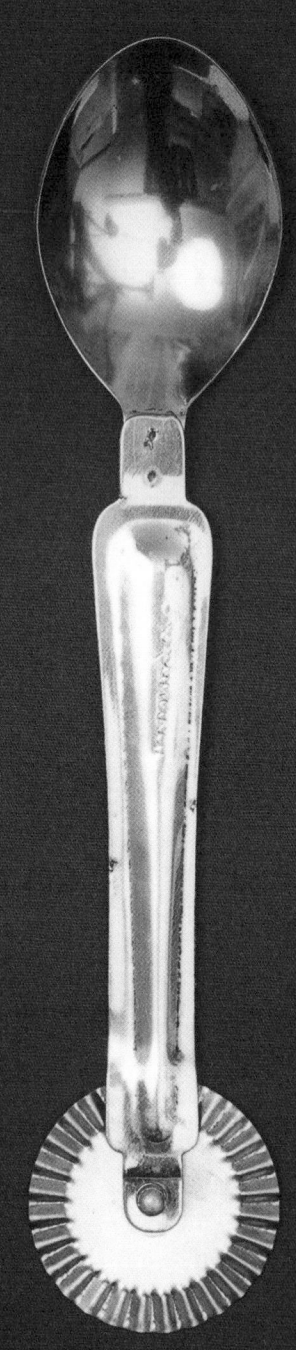

Dual-function spoon
Stainless steel
7 1/4 in. (18.5 cm)
Delhi, Turkman Gate, February 2001
This spoon's handle is endowed with a small wheel. Although we were never able to profit fully from the advantages of this combination, a block of halvah, for example, could be sprinkled with crushed pistachio before being cut into squares with the wheel.

Spoons
Anodized aluminum
3 5/8–4 1/8 in. (9.3–10.5 cm)
Mumbai, Mohamed Ali Road, April 2003
These little spoons, in the colors of the rainbow, are exceptional. We have never seen any like them before: They come from a very special lot. They don't hold up well to daily use and are probably designed only for special occasions: to eat ice cream, perhaps, or to serve the mixture of sugar and fennel grains offered to guests at the end of a meal.

Spoons
Stainless steel
3 1/8–10 1/4 in. (8–26 cm)
Bangalore, SN Raja Road, February 1999; Jaipur, Tripolia Bazaar, February 2001

Food containers
Stainless steel
3 1/2–11 3/4 x 3 7/8–4 7/8 in. (diameter) (9–30 x 10–12.5 cm)
Delhi, 1999; Ajmer, Naya Bazaar, January 2001
These containers, used to transport food, were formerly shaped from tin but today are made of aluminum
(for the less costly version) or stainless steel. The largest is often used to carry oil, milk, or yogurt home
from the shop where it was purchased.

Divided tray
Stainless steel
12 3/8 x 12 3/8 x 1 1/8 in. (31.5 x 31.5 x 3 cm)
Bangalore, SN Raja Road, February 1999
This *thali* tray is used as a plate. Each of the dishes that comprise the meal is served in its own compartment: lentils, rice, soup, pickles, vegetables, dessert. These trays are quite common in working-class restaurants and cafeterias.

Stainless-steel plate
Stainless steel
1 1/8 x 7 3/4 in. (diameter) (2.5 cm x 19.5 cm)
Ajmer, Naya Bazaar, February 2001
Like many Indian objects, this plate serves a variety of functions. It is mainly used to serve salted and spiced delicacies, which Indians are wild about: chickpeas, seeds, peanuts, almonds, and little cakes. They're also often used as covers for water jars, but rarely used as plates.

Plates and bowls
Stainless steel
Plate/covers: 1 3/4–2 3/4 x 8 1/8–9 5/8 in. (diameter) (4.5–7 x 20.5–24.5 cm)
Bowls: 1 3/4–2 3/4 x 6 1/4 in. (diameter) (4.5–7 x 16 cm)
Ajmer, Naya Bazaar, February 2001

Salt and pepper shakers
Stainless steel
3 x 1 1/2 in. (diameter) (7.5 x 3.8 cm)
Mumbai, Kalbadevi Road, April 2003

Thali bowls
Stainless steel
1 5/8 x 3 1/8 in. (diameter) (4 x 8 cm)
Mumbai, Kalbadevi Road, April 2003

Salt and pepper shakers were brought to India by the British; traditionally, guests don't season their food themselves. Bowls are set on a platter and filled with an assortment of dishes (rice, lentils, vegetables, pickles, yogurt, and so on) to make up a complete individual meal.

Pot
Tinned copper, engraved and painted
$3\,^{7}/_{8}$ x $5\,^{1}/_{8}$ in. (diameter) (10 x 13 cm)
Mumbai, Null Bazaar, April 2003
This pot is used for prayers. Although it is not in the least valuable, it was made by an artisan who, by dint of a series of operations, was able to produce a rather refined object: The engraving reveals the copper under the tin, and the painting picks out the floral design.

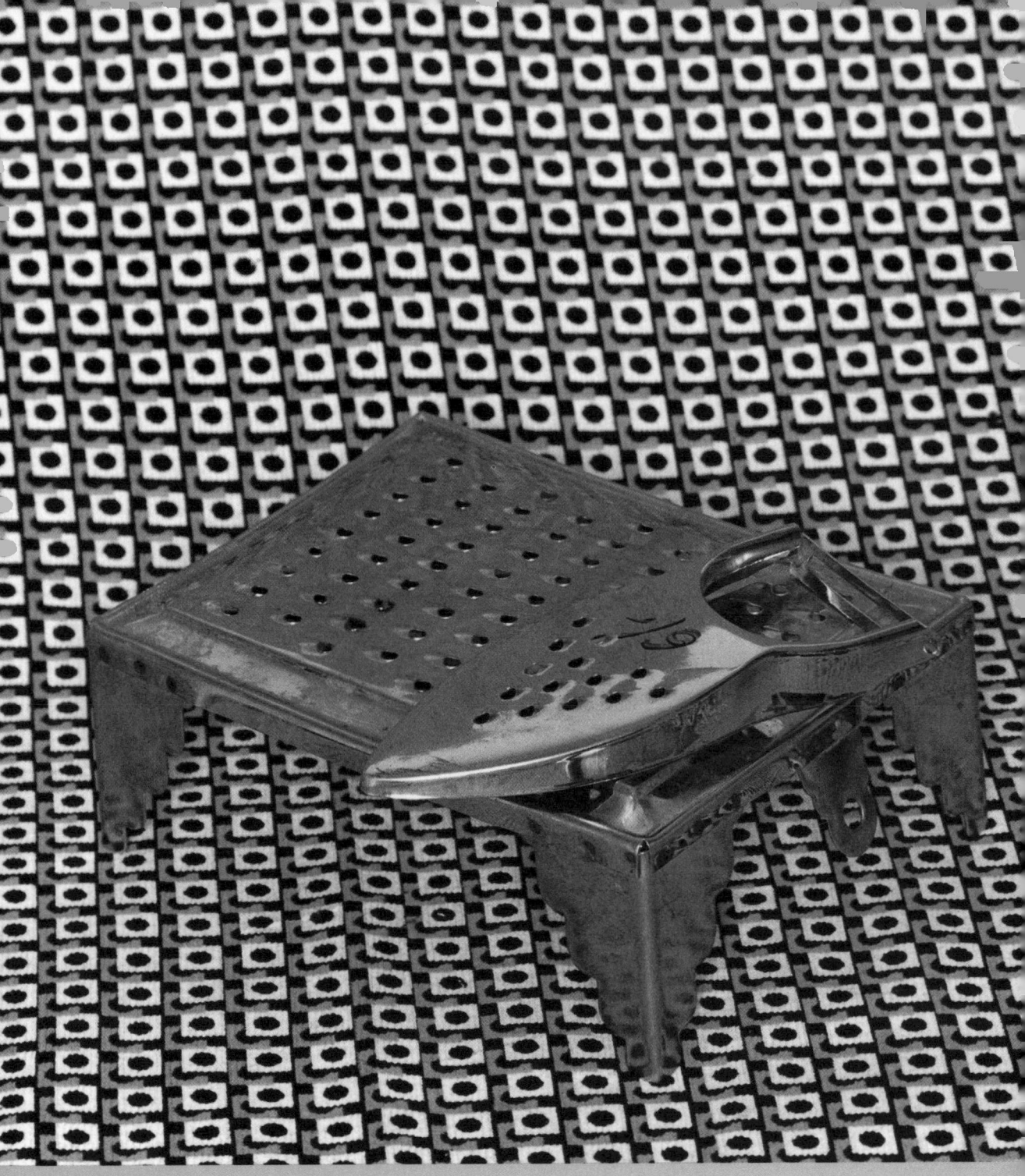

Graters
Stainless steel
4 7/8 x 2 in. (12.5 x 5 cm)
Mumbai, Null Bazaar, April 2003
These graters are used for coconuts, big, bright-green gourds, and various other produce. The little
one is also a peeler.

Coconut board
Wood, laminate, metal
9 $7/8$ x 4 $7/8$ x 3 $3/4$ in. (25 x 12.5 x 9.5 cm)
Mumbai, Null Bazaar, April 2003
If you need to cut up and grate a coconut, it's much easier to use a setup like this. Coconut boards are made in different sizes—this one is unusually small—and of course with different decorations. People usually sit on the board and use a knee or foot as a brace against the effort required to grate the flesh with the jagged disk. The blade is used to cut the nut into pieces.

Lemon press
Painted cast aluminum
6 3/4 x 2 x 2 in. (17 x 5 x 5 cm)
Mumbai, Null Bazaar, April 2003
This object is used for the Indian variety of lemons—which are the size of walnuts. Its color is quite
surprising in a cooking tool, and its weight is very impressive. In India, heaviness—contrasting with the
inherent lightness of "no-good junk," due to skimping on materials—is often thought to be synonymous
with longevity and quality.

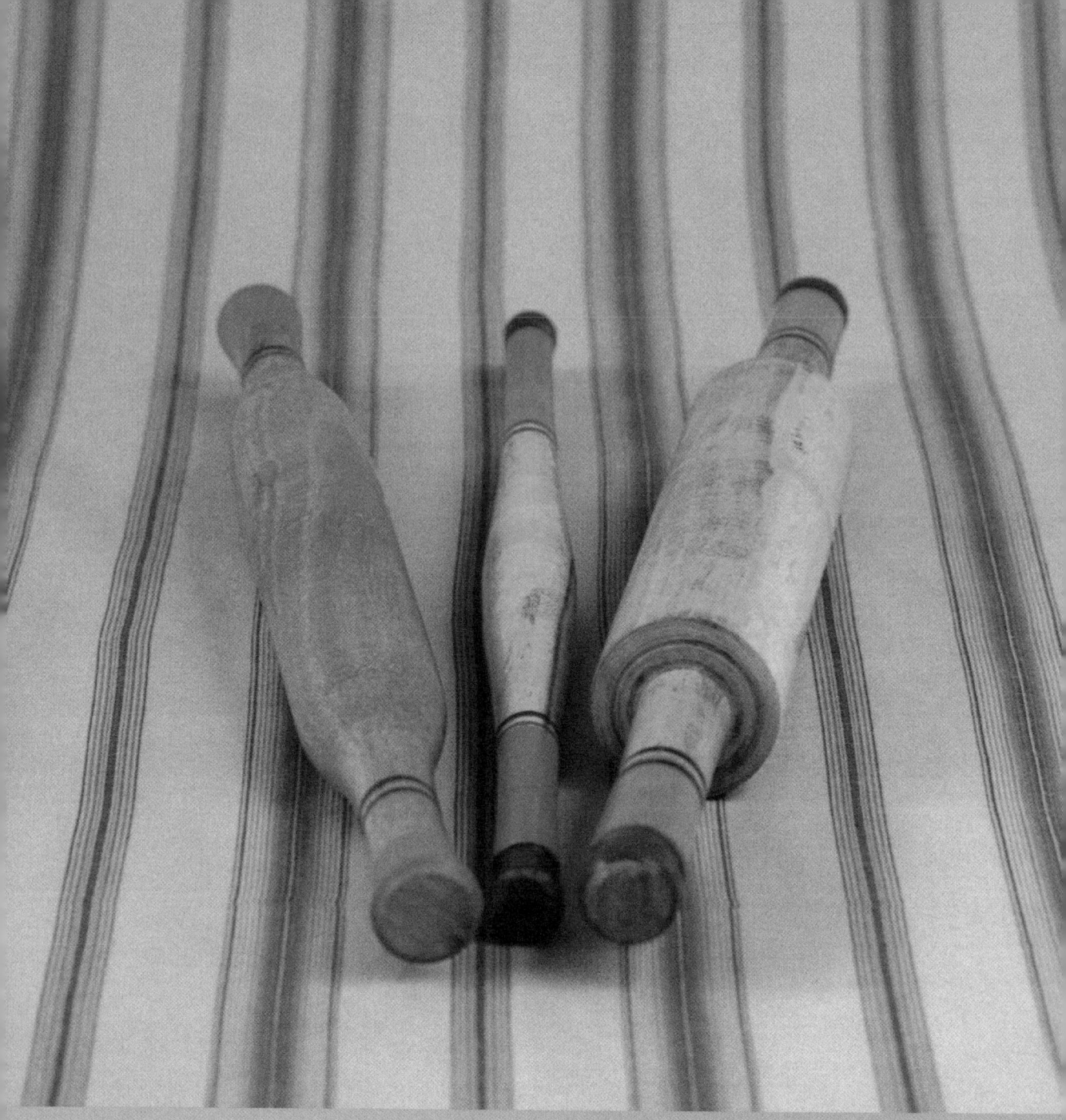

Chapati rollers
Painted wood
14–14 $3/4$ x $3/4$–1 $5/8$ in. (diameter) (35.5–37.5 x 2–4 cm)
Mumbai, Null Bazaar, April 2003
These rollers, usually used on a round wooden platter with various patterns, are essential for making *chapatis*, little pancakes made on the spot for every meal and cooked over the flames as they are needed; the flour (wheat or corn) used varies from region to region. Every household has a roller like these. Indians themselves admit that it takes an exceptionally steady hand and daily practice to make good, round, flat *chapatis* with the most traditional design (middle).

Chapati roller
Stainless steel
13 1/8 x 1 in. (diameter) (33.3 x 2.5 cm)
Jodhpur, February 2001
This roller is an innovative and rather luxurious stainless-steel version of the traditional wooden model.

Glasses
Engraved, molded, blown, and painted glass
$2^{3}/_{8}$–$4^{1}/_{2}$ x $1^{5}/_{8}$–$2^{3}/_{4}$ in. (diameter) (6–11.5 x 4–7 cm)
Jaipur, Tripolia Bazaar, February 2001; Mumbai, Saifee Jubilee Street, April 2003
Because the time invested in decorating things always brings a good return, glasses are very often
engraved with floral or geometrical designs that give them a refined look—even if the foot is sometimes

a little crooked or the finish of the rim is somewhat crude. The slightly flaring shape or the colored edging attracts the buyer's attention, and such a feature may land them on someone's knickknack shelves. The little Eco glasses, copied from an ordinary cafeteria glass, necessitate a rather considerable investment to acquire an injection mold, but they are perhaps bathed in the aura of success they found in Europe. They are often used for serving crushed ice topped with multicolored syrups.

Sorbet glasses
Engraved, gilded, and painted glass
3 1/8 x 2 3/8 in. (diameter) (8 x 6 cm)
Mumbai, Chor Bazaar, April 2003
These glasses are used for syrups, sorbets, fruit juices, and liquor.

Chai glasses
Molded glass
4 1/4 x 1 3/8 in. (base diameter) / 2 1/2 in. (rim diameter) (10.7 x 3.5 cm / 6.5 cm)
Jaipur, Tripolia Bazaar, February 2001
These glasses circulate all day long in little baskets of woven iron wire, full of *chai* or empty. Glasses of *chai* call for the services of a young delivery boy, who drops them off in the neighboring shops on a regular basis, and collects the empty glasses later. The remarkable flared profile is unexpectedly stable and allows for rapid cooling of the liquid contents, making it possible to hold the glass without burned fingers. It also ensures an optimal fit in the basket.

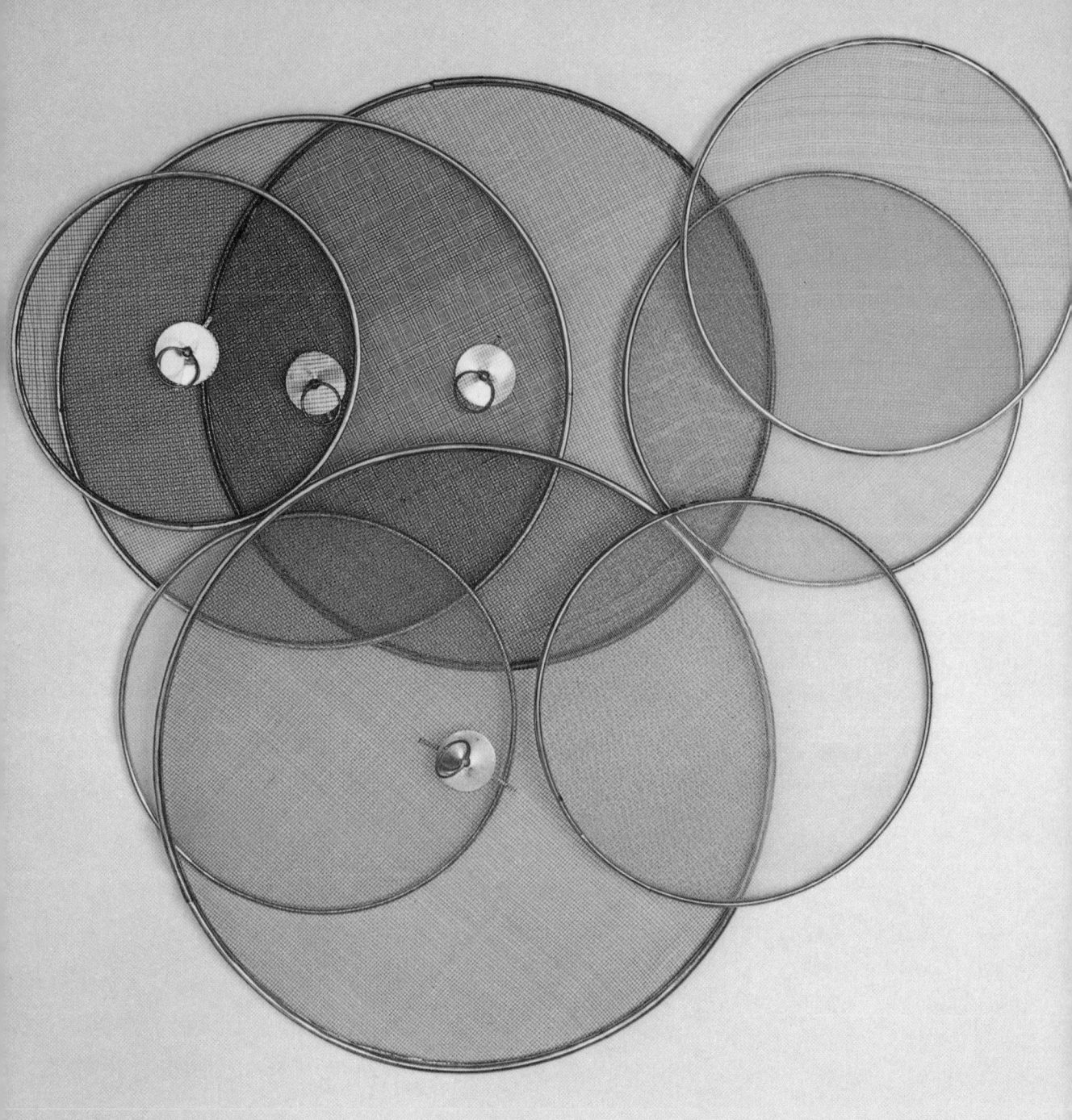

Anti-insect covers/strainers
Metal and synthetic mesh
5 $^7/_8$–10 $^7/_8$ in. (diameter) (15–27.5 cm)
Mumbai, Null Bazaar, February 1999; Jaipur, Tripolia Bazaar, February 2001
These covers protect food from insects.

Kulfi molds
Aluminum
2 1/8–4 3/8 x 1 1/8–2 in. (diameter) (5.5–11 x 3–5 cm)
Delhi, Connaught Place, February 1998
Kulfi is an ice cream made from highly sweetened condensed milk, which is reduced over a low flame and thickened with almonds, saffron, and other spices. Once it is done, it is poured into these molds to make individual servings, traditionally cone shaped.

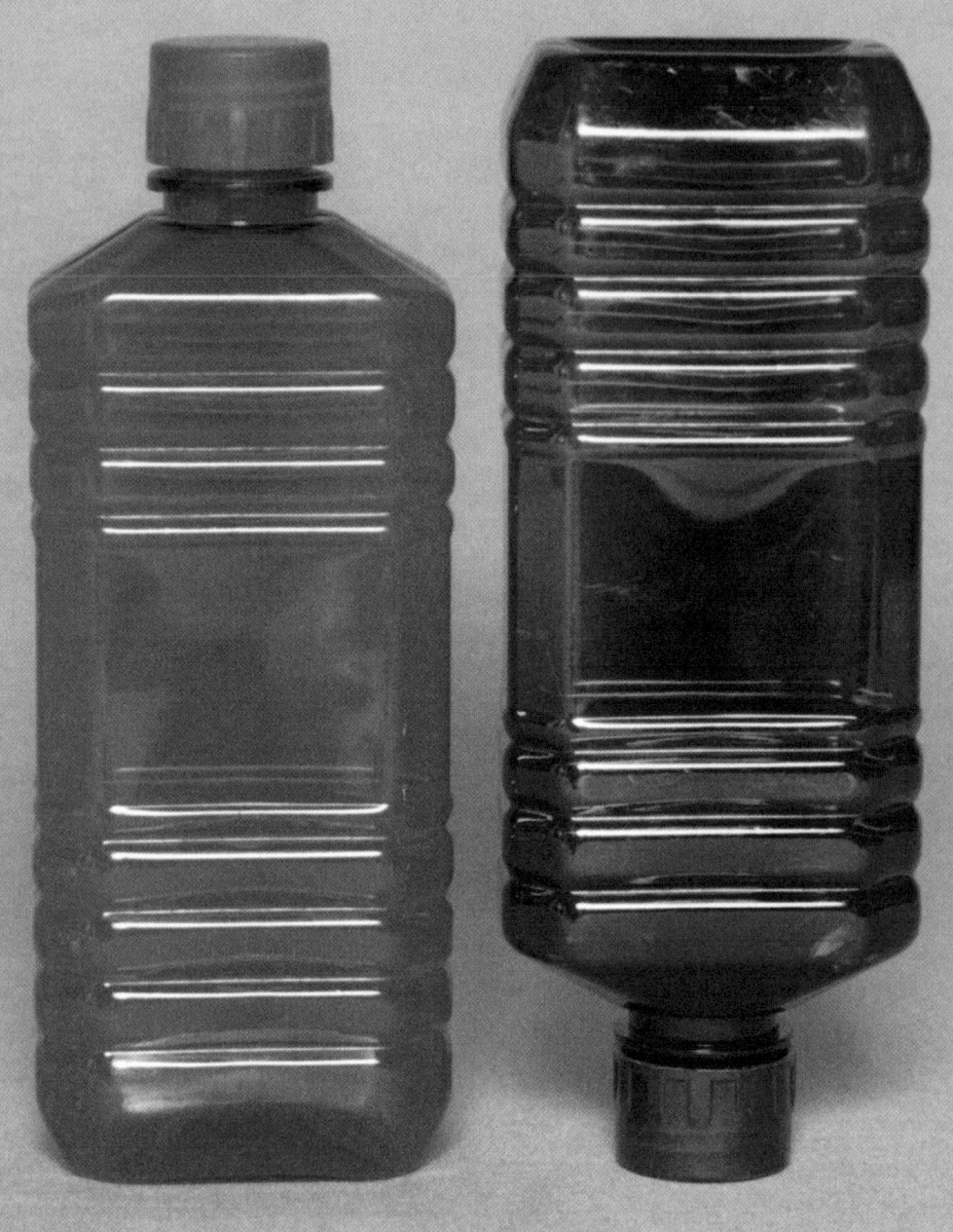

Bottles
Plastic
7 1/4 x 2 3/4 in. (18.5 x 7 cm)
Ajmer, February 2001; Mumbai, Null Bazaar, April 2003
Because the purity of Indian water is often suspect, households usually have a filter attached to the faucet, which allows water consumption without risk. People usually take a full bottle with them when they leave the house, which allows them to avoid the expense of buying mineral water in the street when they're thirsty. These two examples are luxuries, however, because recycled water bottles are perfectly adequate.

Sweetmeat molds
Plastic
Triangle: 1 x 4 3/4 in. (diameter) (2.5 x 12 cm)
Small models: 2 x 1 1/8 inch (5 x 2.7 cm)
Half-moon mold: 3 1/8 x 5/8 inch (8 x 1.5 cm)
Mumbai, Colabra, April 2003
These little gadgets, injection molded in rather thick plastic, are sold right on the sidewalk or in fancy-goods stores in the bazaars. Kitchen tools of attractive colors, they represent a bit of a luxury in Indian kitchens, where most of the basic, serious tools are made of metal. Nonetheless, they work wonderfully well, producing lots of filled and sweetened cakes, marvelously uniform, destined to accompany the most diverse festive occasions. They are today more often used in the villages, since it's easier to buy the cakes ready made, if you can afford them: Every city, even a small one, has its sweetmeat sellers.

Chocolate mold
Colored silicone
5 7/8 x 3 7/8 x 1/2 in. (15 x 10 x 1.2 cm)
Mumbai, Crawford Market, April 2003
Of course, chocolates spring not from Indian traditions but from Western tastes. For this reason, it is considered elegant to make chocolates oneself, especially because the concept of homemade delicacies is beginning to interest the wealthy.

Cake molds
Stamped, or folded and welded aluminum
4/5 (thickness) x 2 3/4 x 1 5/8–3 1/8 in. (diameter) (or 7 7/8 in. for diameter of flower-, star-, and clover-shaped molds) (.2 x 7 x 4–6 cm or 20 cm)
Mhow, Indore and Calcutta, February 2000; Mumbai, Crawford Market, April 2003
The shapes of these cookie cutters are amusing and surprising: stars, airplanes, automobiles, or pine trees (still uncommon in the local landscape): The British brought with them shared, family-size cakes, like sponge cakes and other puddings, but, in India, sweets were traditionally individually served, presented as little minutely crafted mouthfuls. The mold with six blunt points is the only one that has been stamped (from very thick aluminum): It is specially made for the confection of jellies.

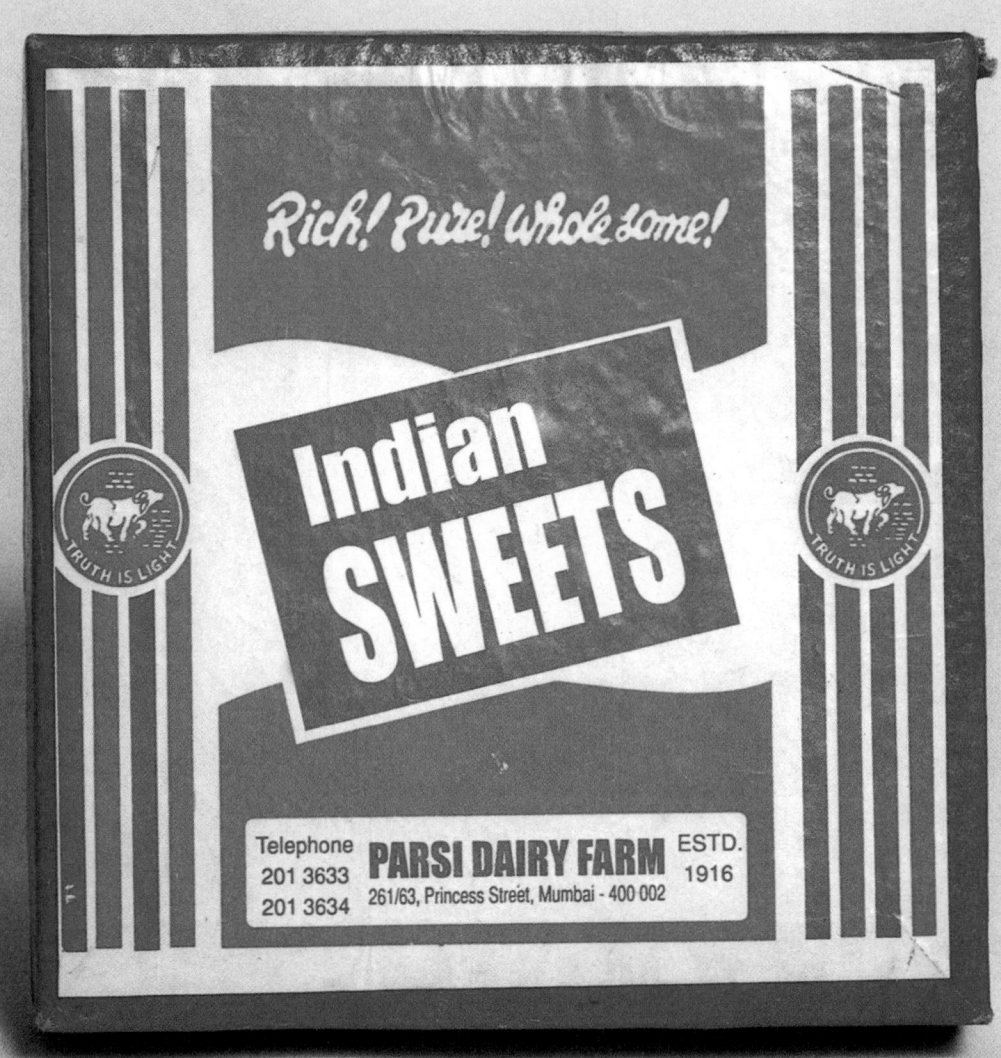

Box for sweets
Cardboard and paper
5 7/8 x 5 7/8 x 2 in. (15 x 15 x 5 cm)
Mumbai, Princess Street, April 2003
This box contains very pretty little traditional cakes, called *mithai,* made from highly sweetened milk and cooked over a slow fire for hours. Of course, spices and other ingredients are added, depending on the nature the cake; they're then decorated like jewels, with silver leaf, filaments of saffron, fragments of pistachio, and so on. At the time of feasts like Diwli they are bought specially for the occasion and presented as gifts in metal boxes decorated with divinities.

Spool of printed ribbon for sweets
Cardboard and paper
5 7/8 x 3 7/8 in. (15 x 10 cm)
Calcutta, February 2002
This garishly colored ribbon, on which the word *Welcome* is repeatedly printed, is used on boxes of
sweets and other goodies.

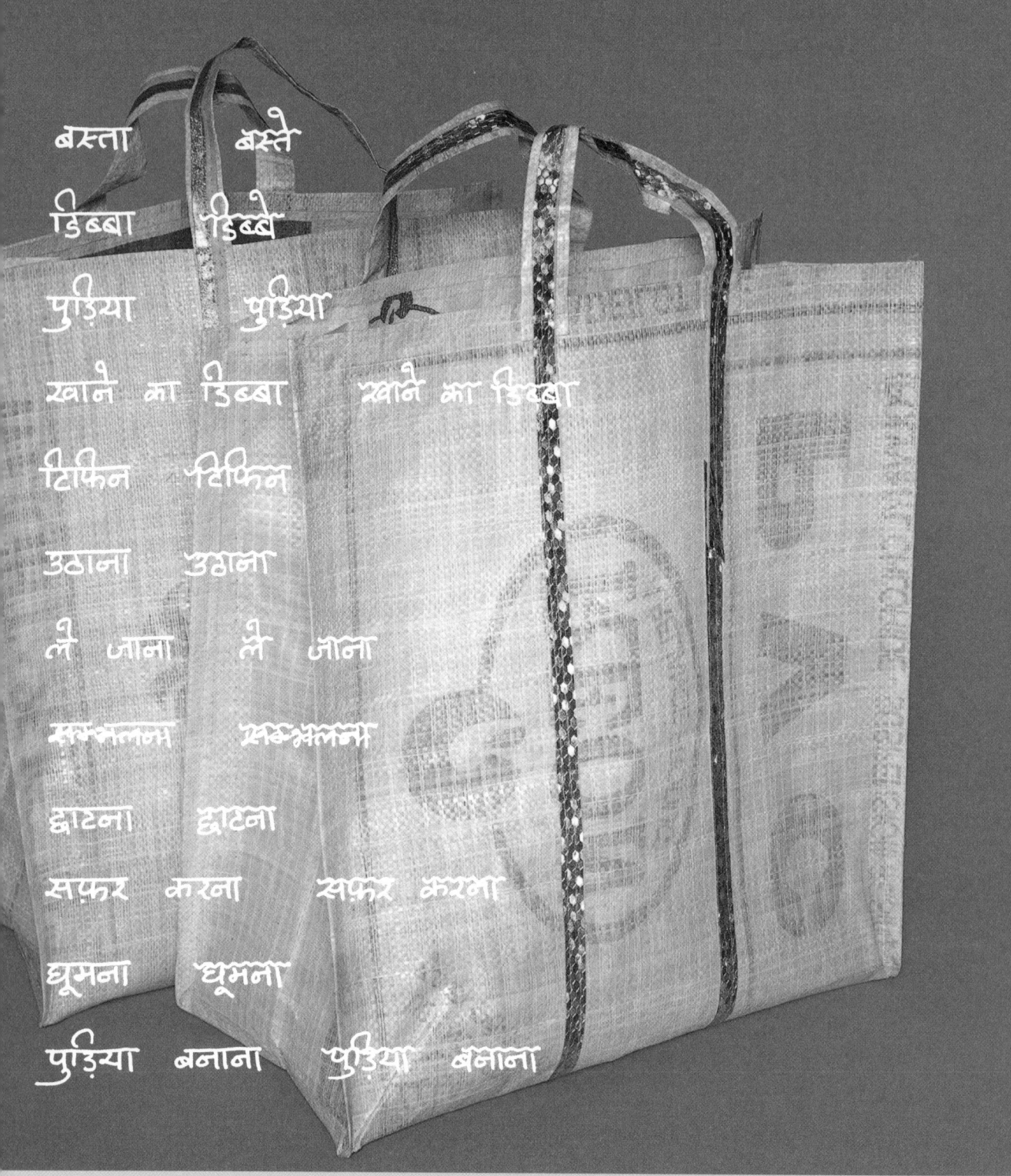

बस्ता — बस्ते
डिब्बा — डिब्बे
पुड़िया — पुड़िया
खाने का डिब्बा — खाने का डिब्बा
टिफिन — टिफिन
उठाना — उठाना
ले जाना — ले जाना
सम्भालना — सम्भालना
ढोना — ढोना
सफ़र करना — सफ़र करना
घूमना — घूमना
पुड़िया बनाना — पुड़िया बनाना

Carry — Transport — Store — Bags —

Select — Protect — Travel — Pack

Boxes crop up all the time in Indian daily life. Are they intended to protect things from the monsoon's humidity, or to keep them out of sight? Without bureaus and bookcases, they serve as a refuge, harboring all kinds of things. There are enormous ones and minuscule ones. In them are stored *paan* (snack wrapped in a betel leaf), lunch, spices, flour, sandalwood powder, *bindis* (the red points Hindu women wear on their foreheads), tools, turbans, saris, jewels, and money. They're made of wood, metal, glass, and plastic, and they're everywhere.

Bags don't do so badly, either. It's hard to keep walking, with everything there is for sale in markets such as Mumbai's Null Bazaar. With the crowded shelves, it looks as if everyone was compelled to drag something from one part of the city to another.

She allowed Roopa and me to open the delicate silver tins still stained with turmeric and vermilion, akshathey and sandal paste from her wedding.

"When you get married," said Ma, "I will fill these boxes with joy, my blessings will perfume each of them."

Anita Rau Badami, *Tamarind Woman*
Chapel Hill, NC: Algonquin Books, 2002

Boxes — Handbags — Lunchboxes

Small boxes
Metal
$3/4$–$2\,3/8$ x $3/4$–2 in. (diameter) (2–6 x 2–5 cm)
Jaipur and Delhi, February 1999; Ajmer, February 1998; Mysore, February 1998;
Mumbai, Null Bazaar, April 2003
The two small aluminum boxes on the far left open on each end. Inside you can store your tobacco on one side and a white lime paste, which improves the flavor, on the other. These ingredients are mixed in the palm of the hand for chewing tobacco. The three little boxes of recycled sheet metal, front left, were bought on the streets. In the center is a tiny box of stainless steel. Front right, the little box of silver, engraved with its owner's name in Bengali characters, contains paste for *bindis*. Back right, two boxes of silver-plated tin originally contained *supari*, or betel nut, a stimulant that is chewed, or grains of cardamom, anise, or other spices. Because these tin boxes vary only in height, the same tooling is used for all the covers.

Tiny boxes
Transparent and opaque pink plastic
$1/2$ x $5/8$ in. (diameter) (1.2 x 1.5 cm)
Pondicherry, February 1996
These boxes are so small that you can imagine them containing a pearl or a baby tooth, or even a precious stone. They can also hold a *bindi*.

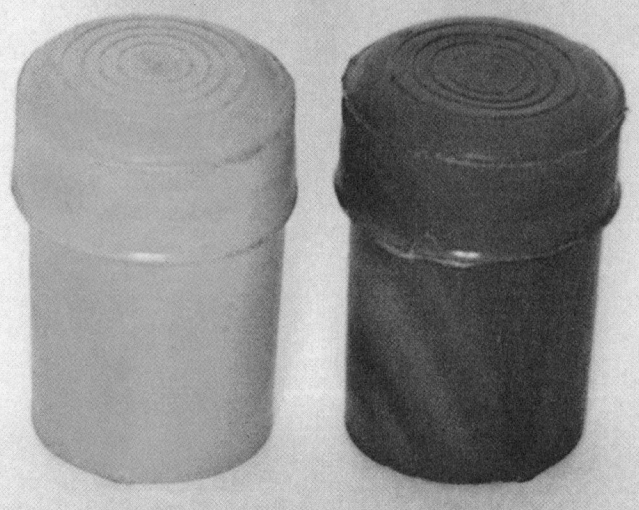

Small boxes
Plastic
1 ³/₈ x 1 in. (diameter) (3.6 x 2.5 cm)
Mumbai, Null Bazaar, February 1999
The lids to these boxes screw on.

168

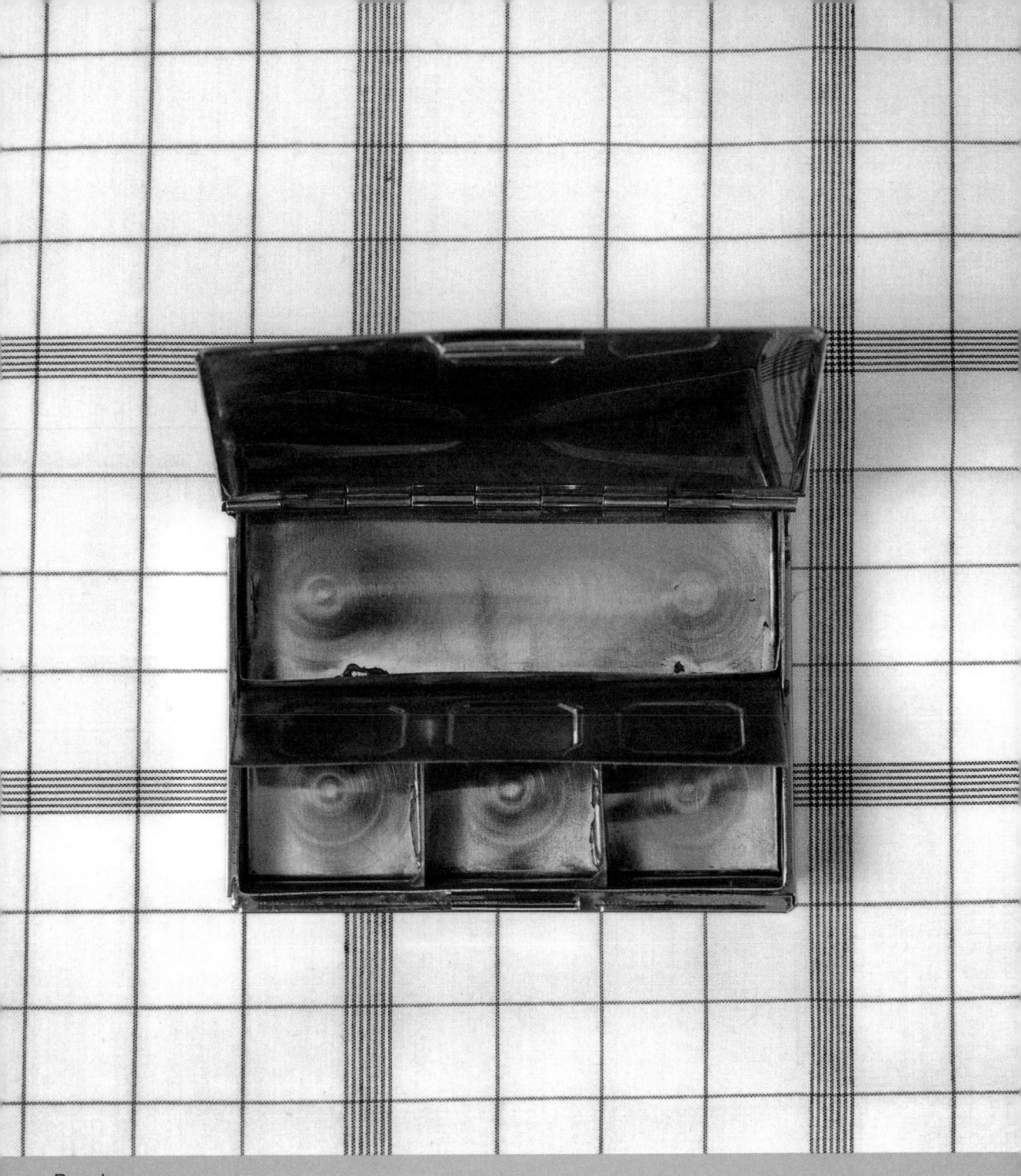

Paan box
Stainless steel
1 1/8 x 3 1/8 x 4 1/2 in. (3 x 8 x 11.5 cm)
Mumbai, Kalbadevi Road, April 2003
This box, with four compartments and two lids, holds and stores all the ingredients necessary to enjoy *paan* and, as an added benefit, is easily hidden in a bookcase, because it's shaped like a book.

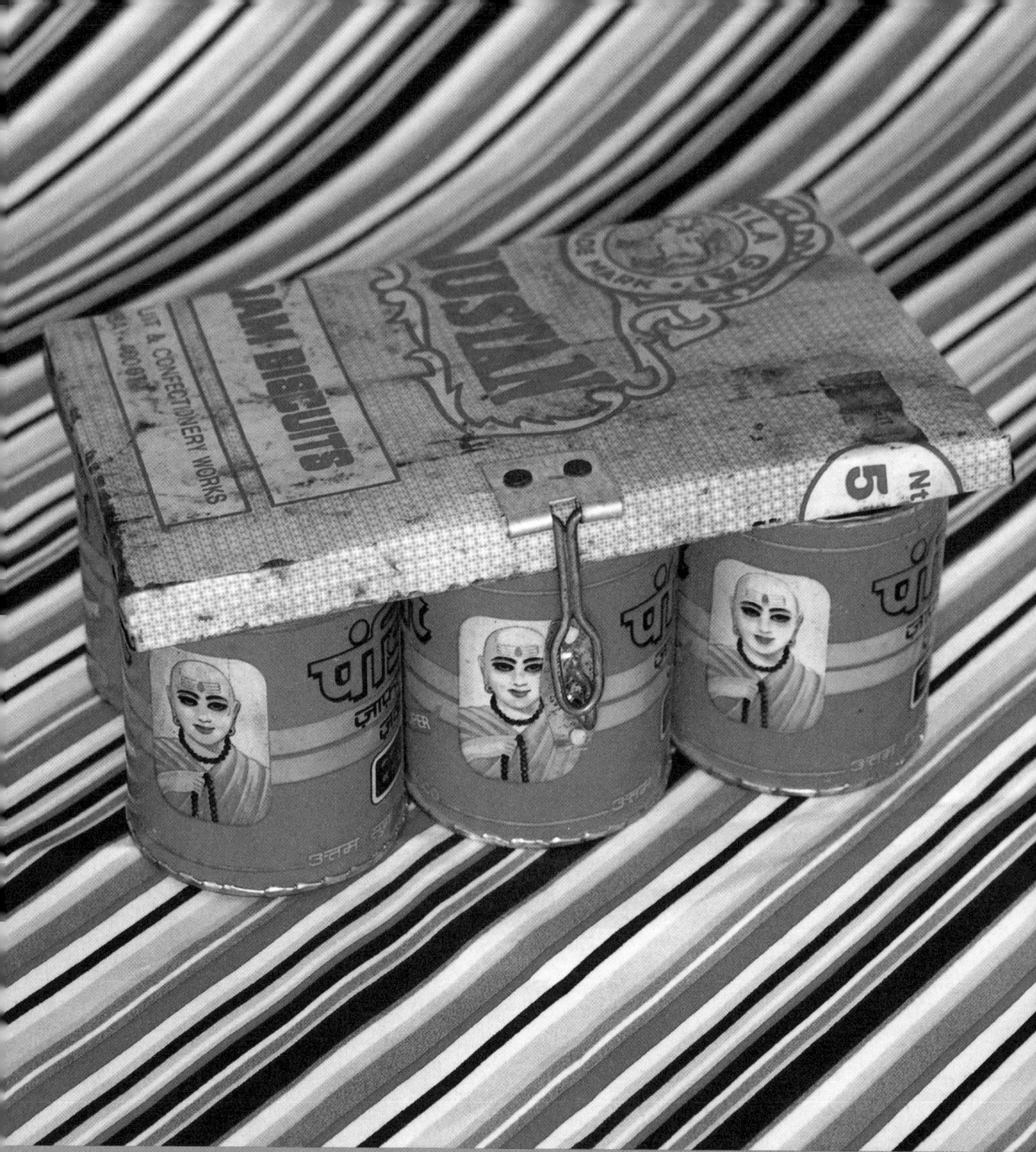

Compartmentalized box
Printed tin
7 7/8 x 5 1/2 x 3 1/8 in. (20 x 14 x 8 cm)
Indore, February 2002
Boxes like this one, soldered together from recycled food cans, are usually sold on the sidewalk in the markets. They're very handy for storing things without having them mix together. A clasp is provided for a padlock.

Box
Bakelite-impregnated cardboard, stamped and
gilt sheet metal
1 5/8 x 2 3/4 in. (diameter) (4 x 7 cm)
Calcutta, Bow Bazaar, February 2002

Box
Embossed and painted tin
2 x 3 7/8 in. (diameter) (5 x 10 cm)
Delhi, February 1999

The box on the left was the usual packaging for bazaar jewelers, who gave them up in favor of those
now found everywhere, their rounded contours covered with imitation red velvet. The one on the right
is a rare find; its Russian-inspired design reminds us of the cordial ties India maintained with the USSR
during the Cold War.

Jeweler's boxes
Cardboard and paper
1 1/8–3 7/8 x 5/8–1 3/8 in. (3–10 x 1.5–3.5 cm)
Ajmer, February 2001
Every purchase from the jeweler, whether a tiny nose ring or something more substantial, deserves to be packed up in a box like one of these, whose interior is lined with fuchsia-colored tissue paper. The lid is usually printed with the store's name and address. These boxes are fast disappearing, replaced by standardized packaging made of plastic, which is considered more fashionable.

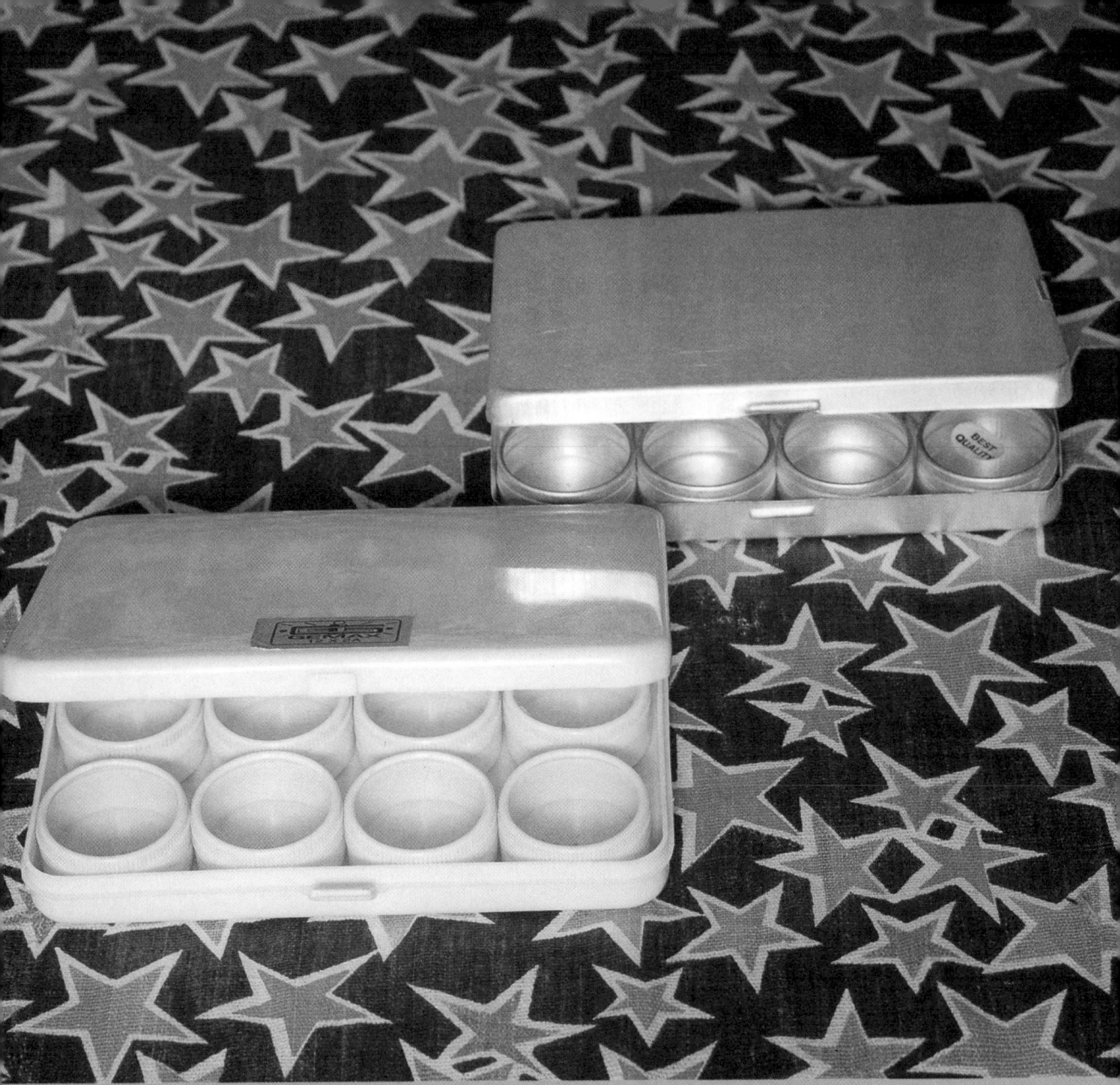

Display box
Aluminum and glass
3/4 x 1 3/8 in. (diameter) (2 x 3.5 cm)
Delhi, Kinari Bazaar, 1999; Jaipur, Gopalji Ka Rasta, February 2001

Display box
Plastic and glass
3/4 x 1 3/8 in. (diameter) (2 x 3.5 cm)
Mumbai, Ghandji Street, April 2003

These boxes are often seen in jewelry shops, where they are used to display precious stones for clients who want to commission a piece. Watchmakers use them as well to hold spare parts used for repairs. They're also used these days to store bindis, and anything else that needs to be displayed.

Flat boxes
Printed tin
$5/8$ x $3\,7/8$–$5\,7/8$ x $3\,7/8$–$7\,7/8$ in. (1.5 cm x 10–15 x 10–20 cm)
Mumbai, Zaveri Bazaar, April 2003
These boxes, made of printed sheet metal originally intended for tin cans, are used by jewelers, who fill them with wax and use them to arrange stones to be set.

Boxes
Aluminum and imitation velvet
Large box: 8 7/8 x 6 1/8 x 2 3/4 in. (22.5 x 15.5 x 7 cm)
Small box: 8 1/8 x 5 1/8 x 2 1/2 in. (20.5 x 13 x 6.5 cm)
Mumbai, Ghandji Street, April 2003
These boxes usually hold jewelry: The velvet protects the contents from damage and provides a
sumptuous presentation.

Boxes
Stamped stainless steel
Left: 5 1/2 x 3 1/2 x 1 3/4 in. (14 x 9 x 4.5 cm)
Right: 5 7/8 x 3 3/8 x 1 3/8 in. (15 x 8.5 x 3.5 cm)
Bangalore, February 1999; Delhi, February 2001
These boxes are used as lunch boxes, for example. The Kissan brand, stamped on the cover of the box on the right, seems to have been borrowed from a large company that makes jams and chutneys. Vegetables are put at one end and rice at the other, and a few *chapatis* (see page 150), wrapped in paper, go on top. Very often, women prepare a meal for their husband at home, whence it is collected and delivered, still hot, by *dabba-wallahs,* who perform this task every day, people say, without ever making a mistake. On the other hand, making meals for others is a not-inconsiderable source of revenue for single women, who this way don't need to leave home to work. They advertise by word of mouth, or through little ads in the newspapers.

Display box
Glass and printed, recycled sheet metal
2 x 4 3/4 x 6 1/4 in. (5 x 12 x 16 cm)
Mumbai, Null Bazaar, April 2003
Portable and lightweight three-dimensional display cases, these boxes are used to present sweetmeats, biscuits, pigments, costume jewelry, spices, beads, and sequins. They're made in different sizes, open at the top, and, of course, can be padlocked shut.

Containers for sweets and spices
Stainless steel and glass
$1^5/_8$–$4^7/_8$ x $1^5/_8$–7 in. (diameter) (4–12.5 x 4–18 cm)
Mumbai, April 2003; Jaipur and Delhi, February 2001
These containers are very popular, because they stimulate the appetite visually even before they have been opened. People put little cakes, peanuts, cashew nuts, and other *chaats* (snacks) inside, safe from insects, rodents, and moisture.

Can of rhodamine dye
Printed sheet metal
2 x 1 ⅝ in. (diameter) (5 x 4 cm)
Jaipur, Tripolia Bazaar, February 2001
These cans contained the pink powder used for prayers and at the feast of Holi, during which everyone
drenches each other with pigments.

Packets

Recycled paper

$3\,7/8-5\,5/8 \times 2\,3/4-7\,7/8$ in. (10–15 x 7–20 cm)

Jaipur, February 1996; Varanasi, February 1999

Although these sachets are made entirely by hand, they aren't really local products, because they may be found from one end of the Indian subcontinent to the other. Made from recycled paper, these containers hold all the small purchases of daily life: grilled peanuts, rubber bands, flower petals, and so on. Because they are often made from the pages of old textbooks, customers often enjoy reading about the fundamentals of religious history or information about the mechanics of reproduction. They are increasingly being replaced by plastic bags, which litter the streets when empty, and which cows munch on with great enthusiasm when they find them.

Bags
Thick cotton canvas, cotton or plastic strap
14 5/8 x 7 7/8 x 16 7/8 in. (37 x 20 x 43 cm)
Jaipur, February 2001; Mumbai, Null Bazaar, April 2003
These bags, originally neither printed nor silk-screened, were used as shopping bags in the big stores:
People filled them with the things they wanted to buy and returned them empty once their purchases
were made. Because they have a large area for display, they were soon covered with advertising extolling
various brands of bidis, Bollywood films, and consumer goods. Then enterprising traders imported them
to the great cities of Europe, where they became very fashionable. Very useful for shopping—the inside
is lined with waterproof plastic—they were adopted by lovers of the exotic who also had a practical side.
Once Indians realized the depths of this infatuation, they began to produce special series, whose designs
were enlivened with sequins, for this unexpected clientele, and flooded the market with them. The number
on the bag indicates its capacity.

Bag
Plastic fabric
18 7/8 x 12 1/4 in. (48 x 31 cm)
Mumbai, Null Bazaar, April 2003
The enormous bags, originally filled with grain and many other commodities in the wholesale market, are later cut up and reborn as shopping bags for household use.

Shopping bags
Cotton canvas, plastic-coated lining (some with exterior plastic coating)
14 5/8 x 7 7/8 x 16 7/8 in. (37 x 20 x 43 cm)
Delhi and Jaipur, 1999; Jaipur, 2001
This series of shopping bags illustrates the evolution of the object: from raw canvas to a vehicle for advertisement, and from silk-screened promotional images on cotton canvas to photographic-transfer processes on plastic-coated cloth.

Bags
Striped woven plastic
9 7/8–24 7/8 x 7 7/8–15 3/4 in. (25–63 x 20–40 cm)
Delhi and Jaipur, February 1999; Jaipur and Pushkar, February 2001; Calcutta, February 2002;
Mumbai, April 2003; Jaipur and Bangalore, February 1999; Delhi, February 2001
These incredibly joyous bags (today widely imported abroad), because they are easily washed, are
mostly used to transport and deliver food. Each retailer makes it a point of pride to display the full
extent of every design's variations in size and color. It is rare to find two in the same pattern on a shelf.

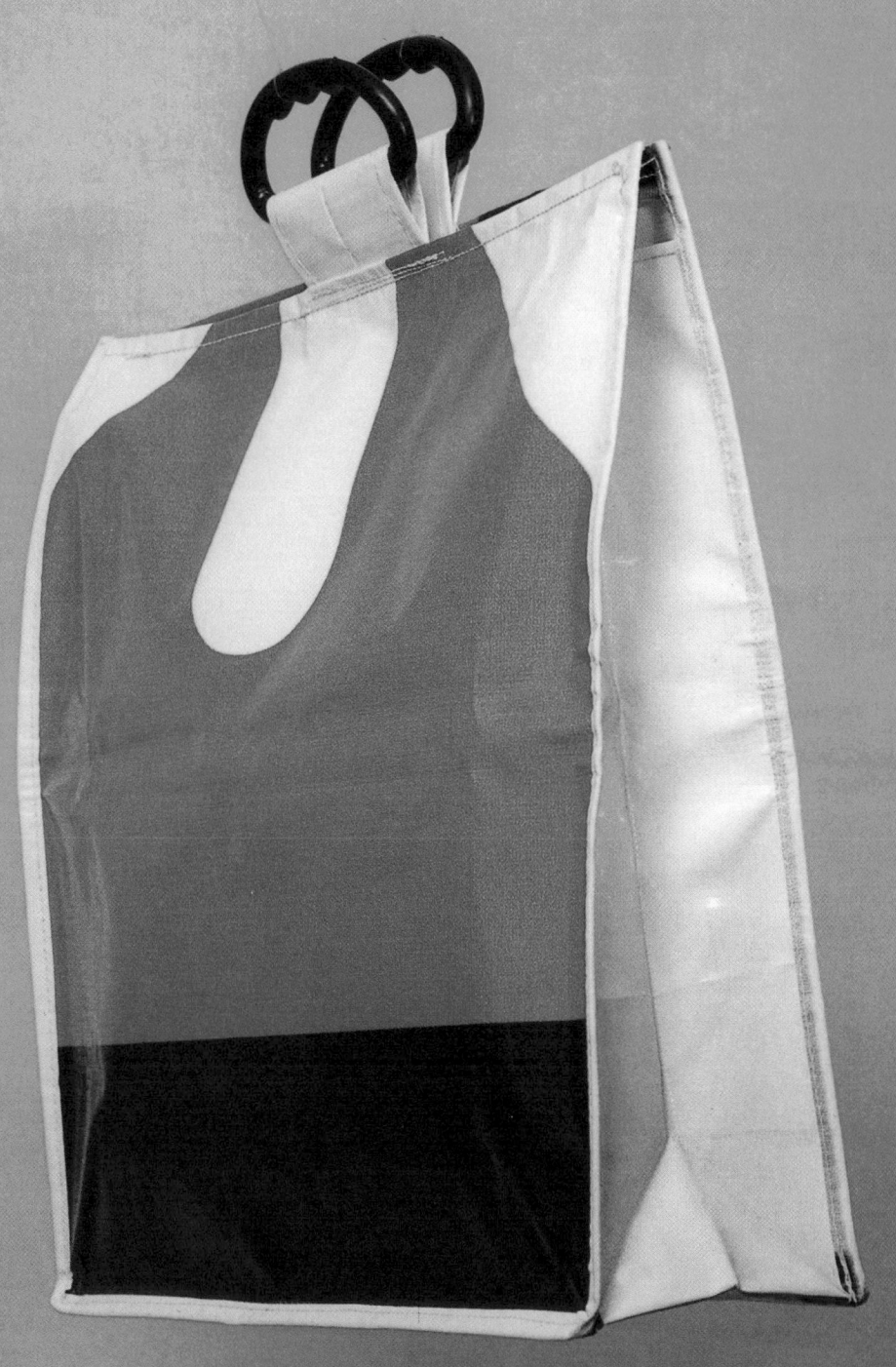

Shopping bag
Waxed canvas, handles of injection-molded plastic
13 3/4 x 5 1/8 x 13 3/4 in. (35 x 13 x 35 cm)
Mumbai, Null Bazaar, April 2003
Although cut from what was once a tarpaulin, this shopping bag—thanks to its attractive ergonomic handles—takes on the look of an elegant handbag.

Bag
Fabric, plastic corners
18 1/2 x 14 1/8 in. (47 x 36 cm)
Jaipur, February 2001
An archetype of the modest and utterly useful Indian bag, which allows you to carry all sorts of things, this shopping bag is made of raw, hand-woven canvas. The corners are made from a recycled plastic bag.

VIP bags
Knitted nylon
18 3/4 x 9 7/8 in. (30 x 25 cm)
Mumbai, Null Bazaar, April 2003
These bags stand out through their original design. The VIP label, displayed on the side, was no doubt scrounged from somewhere; labels are plagiarized on many products throughout India.

Suitcases

Mumbai, Null Bazaar, April 2003

These suitcases, which seem to promise wonderful journeys, are in fact more often used as furniture in which personal possessions are stored—and they are, of course, usually locked with a padlock. The floral or abstract designs seen here are rather unusual. In the bazaar, we often see the conjunction of a purely functional austerity with a highly ornamental disposition.

Suitcase
Painted sheet metal, steel, aluminum, mirror
20 x 11 7/8 x 7 in. (51 x 30 x 18 cm)
Mumbai, Null Bazaar, April 2003
Small suitcases are used for traveling as well as for storage. The interior, often provided with a mirror and a box for valuables, is painted in a color that is a treat for the eyes. In suitcases like this one, young wives carry their trousseau to their husband's house. If she must leave his house, she will carefully padlock it to protect her possessions from the curiosity, and even the greed, of the members of her new family.

Suitcase (open view)

"Come here." Putti pulls me into her room, drags her green tin trunk from under the bed. "I'll show you something." She selects a key from the big bunch that always jangles at her creased waist and opens the trunk. Inside are bags of rupee coins. From heavy silver to the newest stainless-steel ones, a fortune in coins. "Your grandfather is a hypocrite."

Anita Rau Badami, *Tamarind Woman*
Chapel Hill, NC: Algonquin Books, 2002

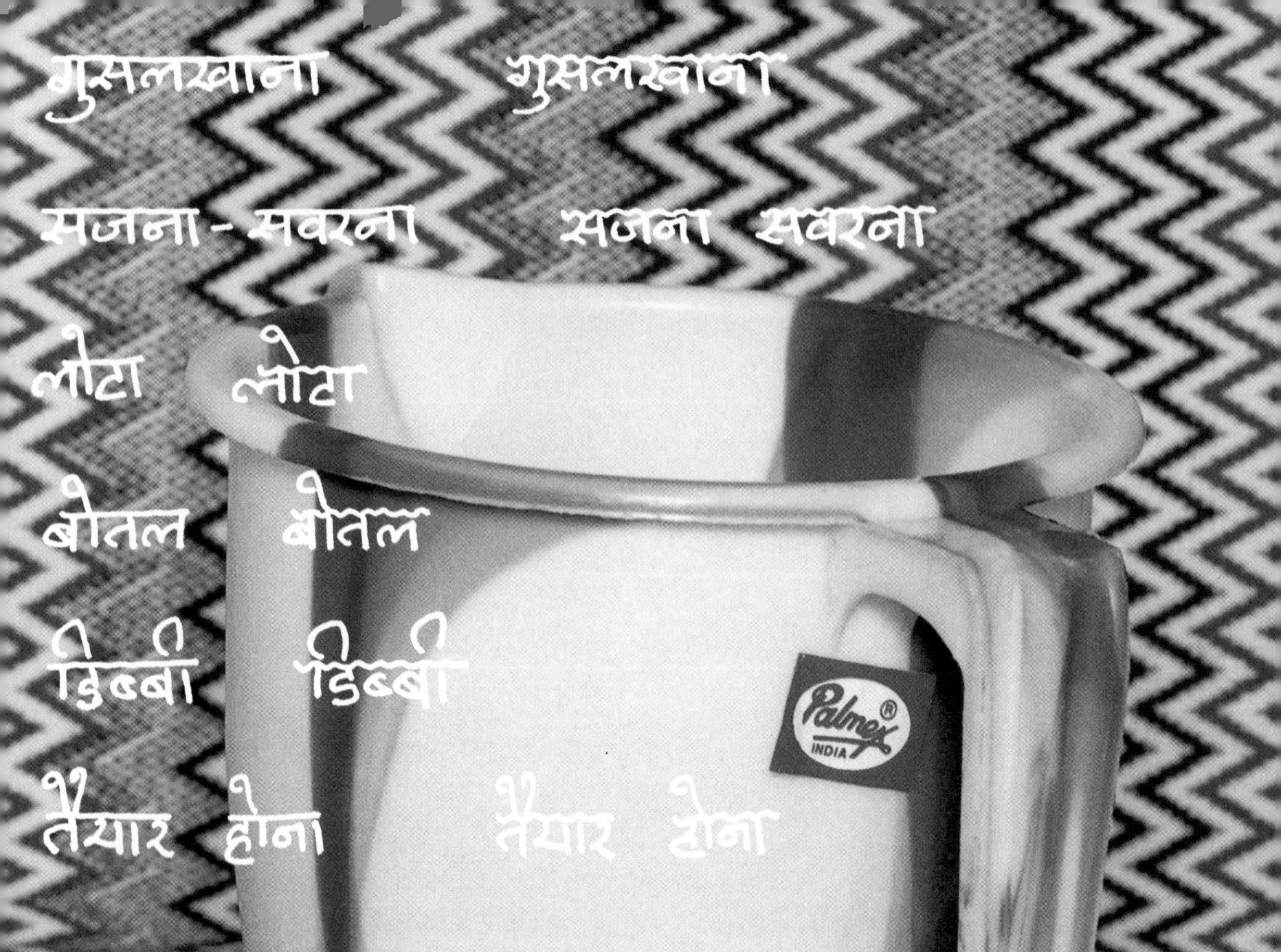
गुसलखाना गुसलखाना
सजना - सवरना सजना सवरना
लोटा लोटा
बोतल बोतल
डिब्बी डिब्बी
Palmex
INDIA
तैयार होना तैयार होना
सजना सजना
बाल बनाना बाल बनाना
शिंगार करना शिंगार करना
शीशा शीशा

Toiletries — Ewer — Jug —

Brush — Makeup — Mirror

India is a country filled with malicious looks and innuendos. Both men and women take pains to protect their image. The cinema industry has strongly influenced people's ways of thinking. Although marriages are often arranged, everyone is secretly longing to discover a passionate, even impossible, love at every street corner. Excessive makeup is frowned on, but the palate of acceptable ornamentation is sufficiently broad that any Indian woman, whether in the cities or in the countryside, can appear like a princess in a fairy tale, dressed in her jewels of gold, silver, or paste, draped in her veils, revealing only her painted toenails or a lock of shining hair. Jewels, bindis, and the material and color of saris often have religious or social meaning. Toe rings, for example, stimulate pressure points and have preventative and curative powers. Medicines are sold at retail stores, and people buy only the number of pills prescribed. The most scrupulous cleanliness reigns: Everyone tries to look their best.

Ma did not fail to notice this generous gesture. As soon as she learned that Baba had parted with a lot of money to buy extra land, she drew up a long shopping list and gave it to her husband.
Two saris to wear at home; Petticoat (white); Blouse (red); A pair of sandals (Bata company); Earrings (long, dangling ones); Glass bangles; Soap; Scented hair oil (Jabakusum); Bar of 570 soap to wash clothes; Soda
Baba raised his eyebrows as he read. "What's this? I bought you a new sari only two months ago!" he said.

Taslima Nasrin Meyebela, *My Bengali Girlhood*
South Royalton, VT: Steerforth Press 1998

Treat — Adorn

Pails and basin
Plastic
6 1/4–12 1/4 x 7–13 in. (diameter) (16–31 x 18–33 cm)
Jaipur, February 2001; Mumbai, Chor Bazaar, April 2003
These large pails are most often found in bathrooms, which are usually equipped only with a shower and faucets. So as not to waste water, the pail is filled and water is drawn from it using a little pitcher. They're also used to haul water when a faucet is shared among several families. In the past, pails were made of aluminum or even stainless steel. Plastic came later, and the brightly colored two-color injection molding appeared later still. This style, however, is today outmoded: Frosted, multicolored plastics, imported from China, are highly prized in the big cities.

Buckets
Injection-molded plastic (varying dimensions)
Mumbai, Chor Bazaar, February 1999
The brightly colored pattern disguises the defects inherent in injection molding, and gives the object an added decorative value.

Pots
Plastic
From $3\,^1/_2$ x $3\,^3/_8$ in. (diameter) (9 x 8.5 cm) to $3\,^7/_8$ x $4\,^1/_8$ in. (diameter) (10 x 10.5 cm)
Chittaurgarh, February 2003

These pots are used for washing and rinsing in the bathroom more than for cooking. Their price is low, and their quality is, too: The plastic is particularly thin and easily dented. They are made in small workshops, sometimes in villages, or in the suburbs of small towns. There are as many molds as there are producers, whence variations in size and shape seen in the same design. This palette of dark colors, produced by mixing a range of colors from previously recycled plastics, is very unusual.

Pitchers

Gray pitcher: 7 $1/2$ x 2 $3/8$ in. (diameter) (19 x 6 cm)

Red pitcher: 9 $7/8$ x 3 $1/2$ in. (diameter) (25 x 9 cm)

These pitchers are used in the kitchen but also in the bathroom—wherever water is poured.

The bathroom needs cleaning. I open a new can of Ajax and scour the tub. Sloshing with mug from bucket was standard bathing procedure in the bathrooms of Firozsha Baag, so my preference now is always for a shower. I've never used the tub as yet; besides, it would be too much like Chaupatty or the swimming pool, wallowing in my own dirt. Still, it must be cleaned.

Rohinton Mistry, *Swimming Lessons and Other Stories from Firozsha Baag*
Boston: Houghton Mifflin, 1989

Liquid-soap dispenser
Plastic and metal
5 1/8 x 3 3/4 in. (diameter) (13 x 9.5 cm)
Delhi, Kotla Bazaar, October 2003
This soap dispenser conjures a world of sparkling cleanliness from which the ever present bar of soap,
swollen with water and dissolving on the edge of the sink, has miraculously been banished.

Hand towels
Cotton toweling
34 5/8 x 18 7/8 in. (88 x 48 cm)
Bangalore, February 1999
These cotton hand towels, of excellent quality, are attired in seductive stripes—sometimes blended and subtle, sometimes bright and lively. They're double sided, as soft on the reverse as on the front. In a store, you never see two towels with the same design; everyone chooses a towel that is unique in some way. Choice is important, and the retailer may buy one of every variety of stripes from the wholesaler, as if taking a survey, so as to offer clients the widest selection possible. This flexibility in purchasing, difficult to manage in Western countries, is still a reasonable commercial approach in India.

Razors
Plastic and metal
2 3/4 x 1 5/8 in. (7 x 4 cm)
Mumbai, Null Bazaar, April 2003
These razors are identical in shape to older, metal models. Their overall performance seems rather doubtful, and you can see flecks of orange in the green plastic, the residue of the color previously injected into the mold.

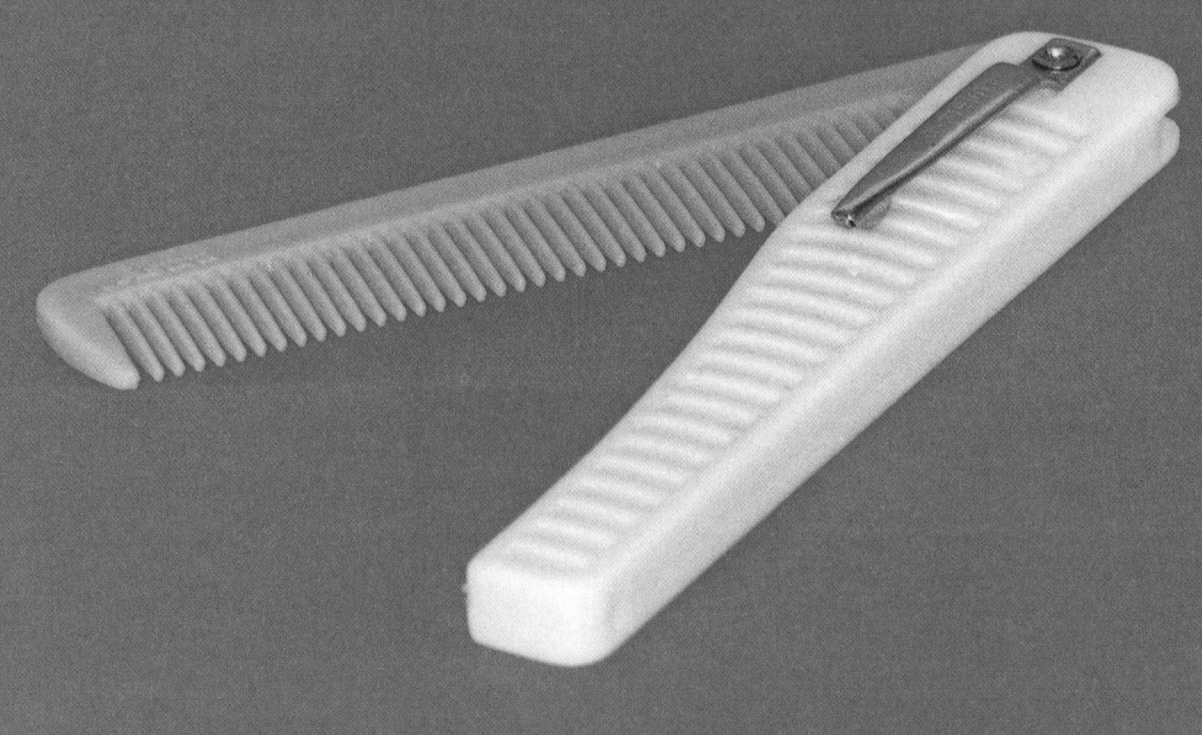

Pocket comb
Plastic and metal
5 $\frac{7}{8}$ x 1 $\frac{5}{8}$ in. (15 x 4 cm)
Mumbai, Mohamed Ali Road, April 2003
Plastic combs are almost always carried by men; women don't fix their hair in public. Because pink has no childish or feminine connotations in India, combs of that color are not out of the ordinary. This comb has two additional advantages: It folds, and, thanks to the metal clip with which it may be attached to a shirt pocket, it can pass for a pen.

Head-lice combs
Plastic inlaid with iridescent plastic
4 1/2 x 2 3/8 in. (11.5 x 6 cm)
Mumbai, Mohamed Ali Road, April 2003
Head lice are common in India, and these combs come in an infinity of forms. These have the look of
real beauty accessories. The inlay work takes a great deal of time and skill, even if it is executed in
low-quality plastic.

Brushes to clean head-lice combs
Metal and plastic
2 1/8 x 1 in. (5.5 x 2.5 cm)
Mumbai, Mohamed Ali Road, April 2003
These little feather dusters of iron wire, with pearly handles resembling candy, are used to clean head-lice combs, and indicate the attention paid to delousing. There's no question of throwing away a comb while it still has life in it; it needs to be maintained with the care it deserves. The savings realized by investing in this little tool are not thought of as trivial.

Sets of barrettes
Painted metal
2 x ⅛ in. (5 x 0.5 cm)
Ahmadabad, February 1999
These rectangular barrettes adorn the shiny black hair of Indian women. In the workshop, they're carefully
lined up, and the stripes are hand painted with a single stroke of the brush, decorating many pieces at
the same time.

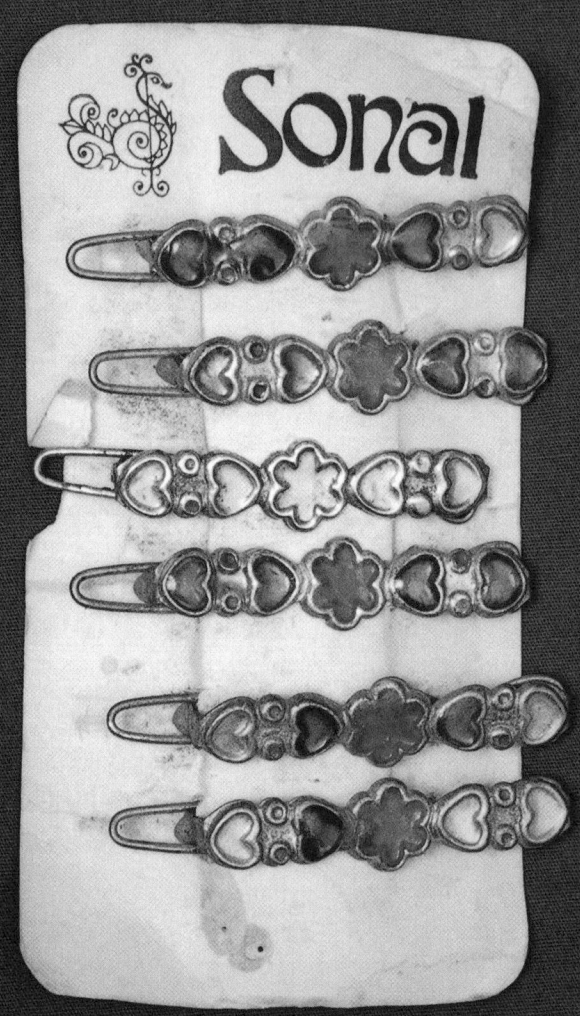

Barrettes
Painted metal
2 x ³/₈ in. (5 x 1 cm)
Mumbai, Mohamed Ali Road, April 2003
The reasons the painting on these barrettes hasn't been finished is unknown to us, and raises many possibilities. Is it to give the client a choice? Is it because the maker ran out of paint? Because the tea was getting cold?

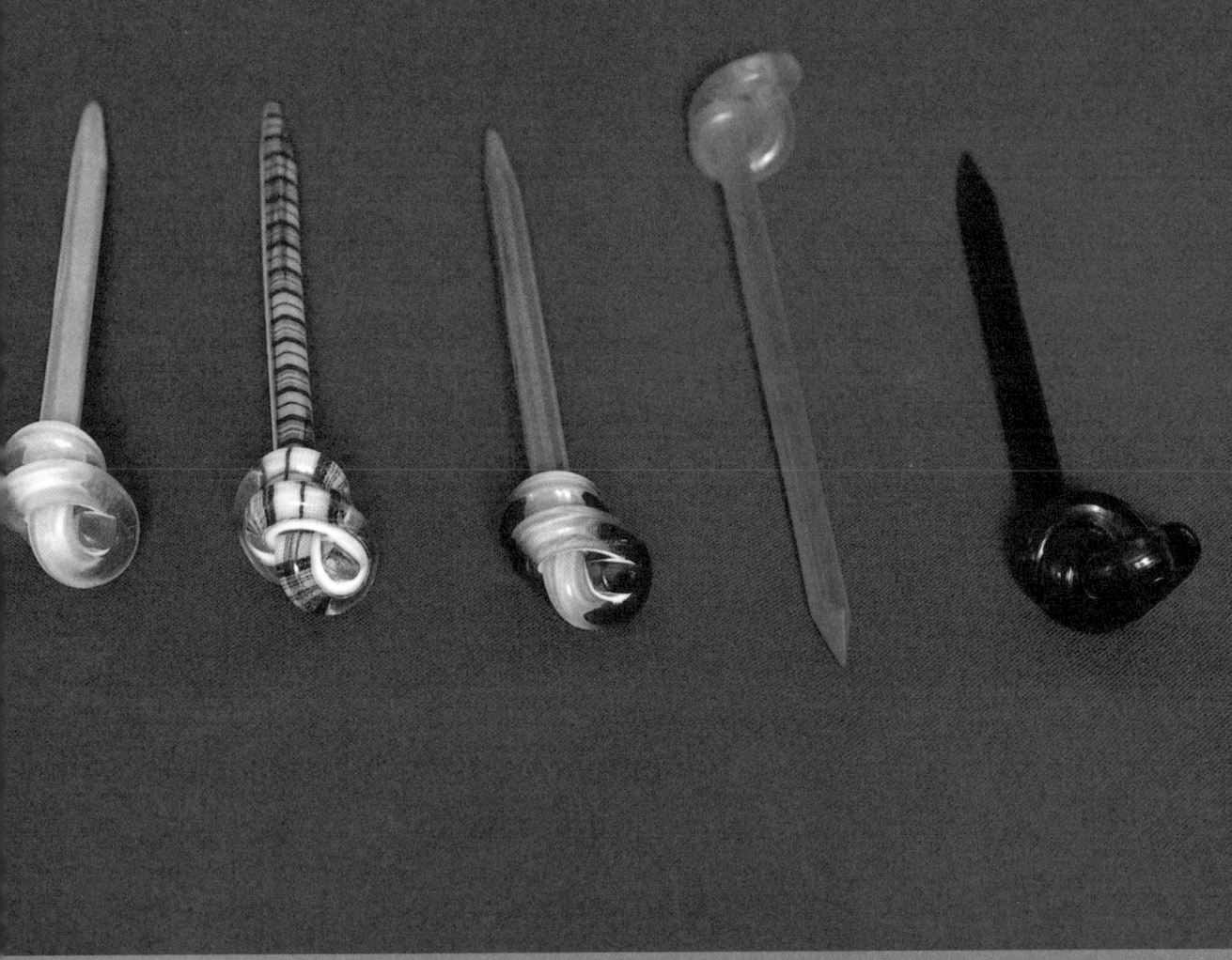

Hair picks
Plastic
5 3/8 in. (13.5 cm)
New Delhi, Lajpat Nagar, April 2003
The points of these hair picks are sharpened like a dagger so they can be set in the thickest hairdo. This lively design is made cheaply, and with a great deal of ingenuity: All you have to do is knot the plastic while it is still warm. The result is stylish, and the knot keeps the pin from sliding through the hair.

Mirror
Glass, plastic
9 x 6 1/4 x 2 in. (23 x 16 x 5 cm)
Jaipur, Sanjay Bazaar, October 2003
Although this mirror is really of the cheapest quality, it fulfills its duties perfectly, and its little folding shelf is very useful.

Various mirrors
Engraved, etched, ground, or painted glass
Frames of stainless steel, tin, or wood
4–7 7/8 x 2–11 3/4 in. (10–20 x 5–30 cm); 5 7/8–1 5/8 in. (15–4 cm) (diameter)
Mumbai, Mohamed Ali Road, February 1999 and February 2001; Dundlod, February 2002

It is rare in India not to have a mirror before which you can arrange your hair, shave, apply a bindi, and so on. The popularity of this article shows how important it is to be well groomed. The example decorated with parrots and little lotus flowers is part of a marriage trousseau. There is no mirror so small as to be despised, and a broken mirror is carefully reshaped by the corner mirror maker; it will not be thrown away, and will rather be cut down until there is only the smallest bit left. This bit, what is more, may be set in an ornate metal frame that will give it new life, because materials are much more expensive than labor. The decoration of engraved balls, as shown in the double mirror (upper right), was, until recently, extremely popular. Any glass worker worthy of the name had the equipment for grinding these lozenges and flowers. Many shops in Mumbai, especially those selling floral essences and paan and cigarettes, are decorated floor to ceiling with these worked and painted mirrors. In the countryside, you often see mirrors set into the facades of buildings. This way, you can take advantage of the light outside to look at yourself; what is more, no one can steal or break them, and, if an evil spirit approaches, it will be scared off when it sees the ugliness of its own reflection.

Box of bracelets
Engraved plastic
8 1/4 x 3 1/2 in. (21 x 9 cm)
Mumbai, Mohamed Ali Road, April 2003

A well-dressed Indian woman rarely goes out without her bangles, or bracelets, which carefully match the colors of her sari. The shades of these accessories vary endlessly, covering a broad enough spectrum so that anyone can find the tones that exactly match. Traditional bracelets are made of glass, or of gold or silver, or sometimes of bone or ivory, but the arrival of plastic on the scene has increased the range of effects: They may be spangled, engine turned, pearly, sparkling, matte, gilt, fluorescent, and so on. Glass bracelets are often sold in the streets from carts on which they're arranged in a circle like a bouquet. They're sold in sets of six, and they're sized very small: Putting them on takes long practice, which consists of squeezing the hand as much as possible so they can slip on without breaking. Presentation boxes, which also come in many versions, let women who are in a hurry take in the whole of a collection with a single glance.

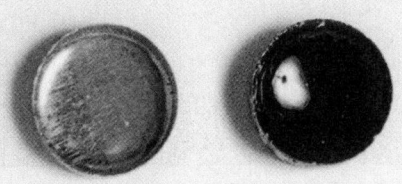

Bindis and bindi paste
Plastic
$3/8-5/8$ inch (1–1.5 cm)
Mumbai, Zaveri Bazaar, April 2003
Bindis are ornaments, usually round and red, that married Hindu women traditionally wear on the forehead. The preferred location—slightly above the eyebrows, extending the ridge of the nose—has given rise to such a proliferation of styles that it would be impossible to list them all here. Materials include gold, diamonds, felt, plastic, and even glass, meticulously painted with gold or pure silver or drawn with a brush in every shape and all the colors of the rainbow. They are glued to the forehead with a sticky substance we were not able to identify, and with which the microscopic container is filled.

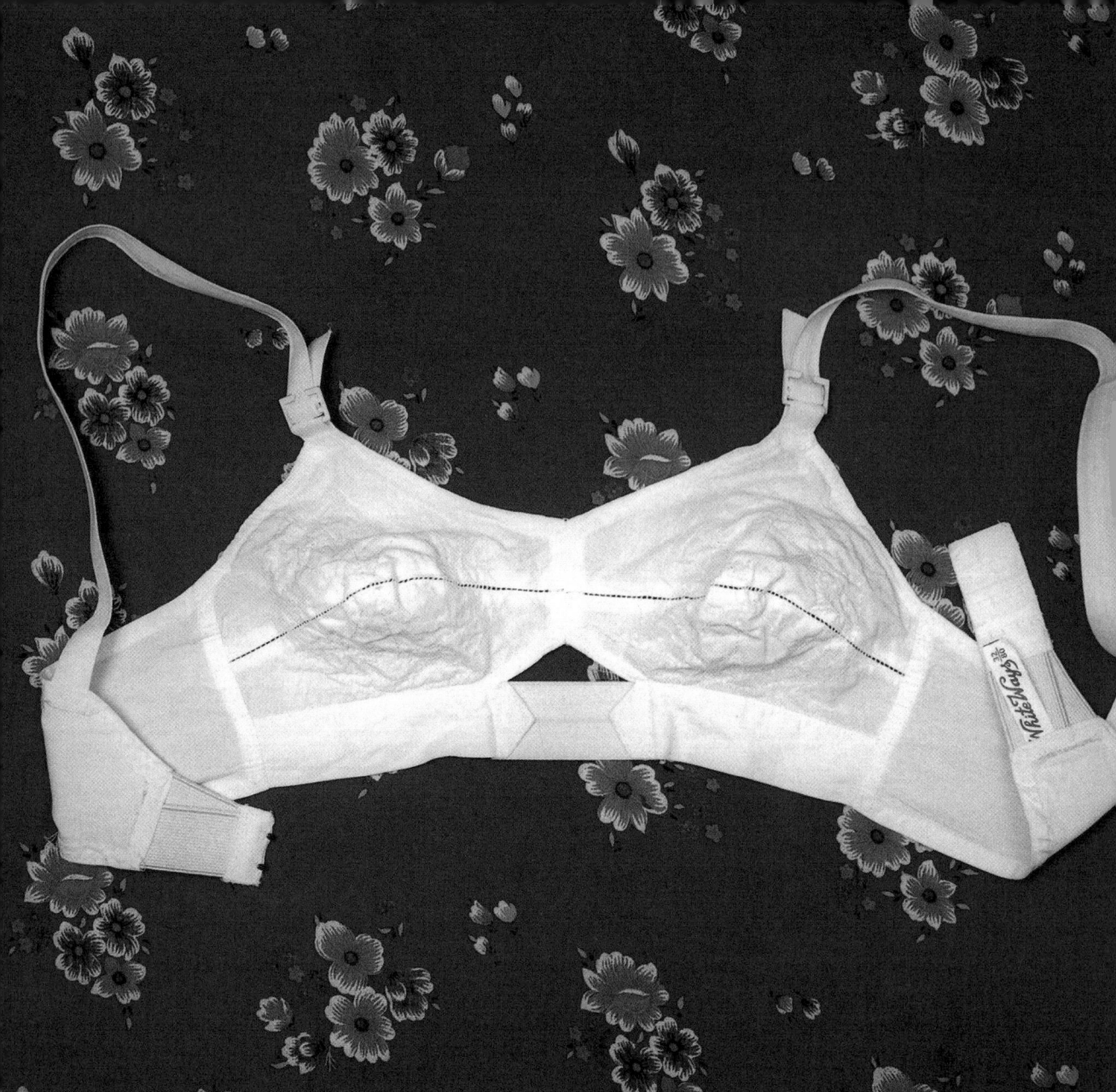

Bra
Cotton
Hyderabad, February 2001

On the sidewalk, before him, like so many hilltops, piles of bras were lined up: red ones, white and black, the colors of Durga, the goddess of illusion.

On the pavement in front of him, like mountain ranges, are rows and rows of brassieres. Red, and white and black, the colours of Durga, the goddess of illusion.

"For Rekha-actress figure, sister!" shouts the man, thrusting his fist to fill the cup and pulling it out again to show how the fabric maintains its shape. . . . "Sister, sister, even when nothing is there, it will give you Rekha-actress figure."

The illusion-monger holds a red bra over his own chest, bare brown, a thin coating of skin stretched over his ribs. . . . "Export quality, sister, suspension like the Howrah Bridge, strong everlasting."

Anita Rau Badami, *Tamarind Woman*, Chapel Hill, NC: Algonquin Books, 2002

Box of Godrej black hair dye
New Delhi, February 2001
3 ³/₈ x 3 in. (8.5 x 7.5 cm)
When the hair turns white under the weight of the years, Indians, especially men, sometimes dye their hair. The choice of colors is fairly limited, of course: You can find black or henna, which, although it strengthens the hair, turns it bright orange.

No boy, he observed with relief, but a man of less than fifty. He could well have bad intentions toward Kajol or Malati. He was the type whose dyed hair was oiled and combed straight back, checkered handkerchief peeking out of his pocket, blue stockings.

Bulbul Sharma, *The Anger of Aubergines: Stories of Women and Food*
New Delhi: Kali for Women, 1997

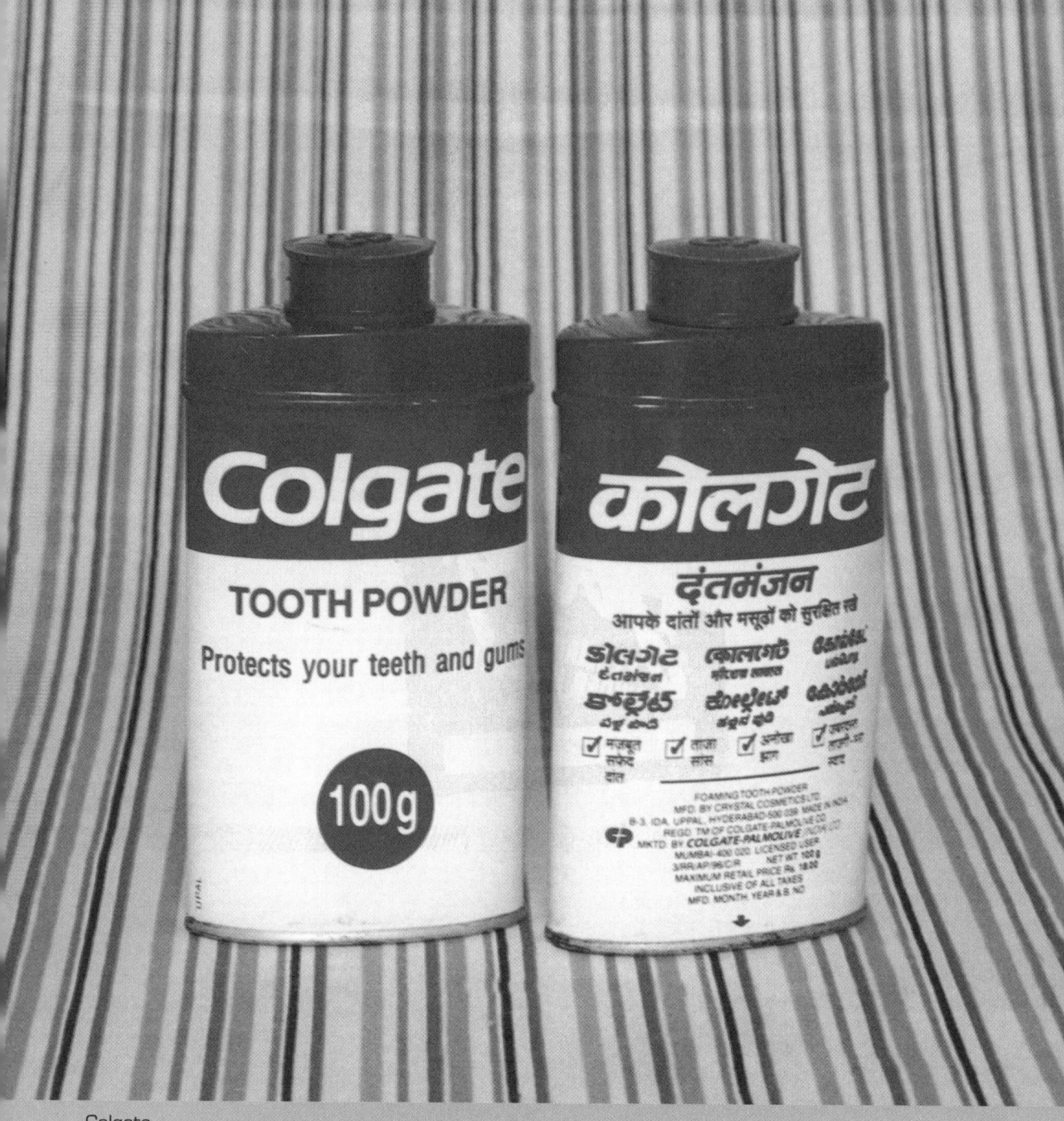

Colgate
Printed sheet metal and plastic
4 ¾ x 6 ¾ in. (12 x 17 cm)

In India, although some people still clean their teeth in the traditional way, with a twig from the *margosa* tree, Colgate brand holds the high ground when it comes to toothpaste. It is often found in powder form, and the different permutations of packaging reveal an attention to the finer points of marketing that is fairly uncharacteristic: The family-size container is decorated with pictures of laughing children against a backdrop of Swiss mountains. Its metal cans, which are giving way to plastic, are the joy of those who are apt to reuse such discarded items, and the many pieces of sheet metal nailed up here and there to plug holes continue to display the trademark red and white in the oddest places.

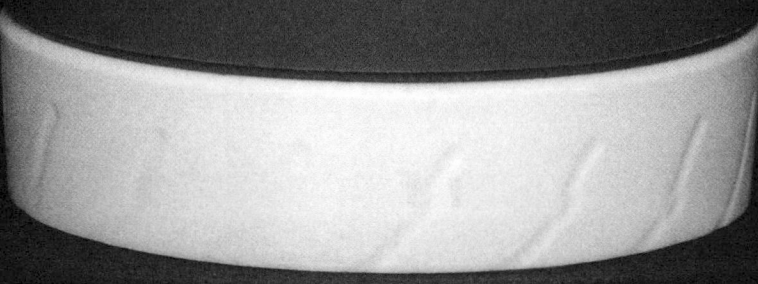

Brylcreem
2 ³/8 x 2 ³/8 in. (diameter) (6 x 6 cm)
Mumbai, Royal Yacht Club, April 2003
This hair cream is supposed to wage a merciless battle against shameful dandruff for twenty-four hours.

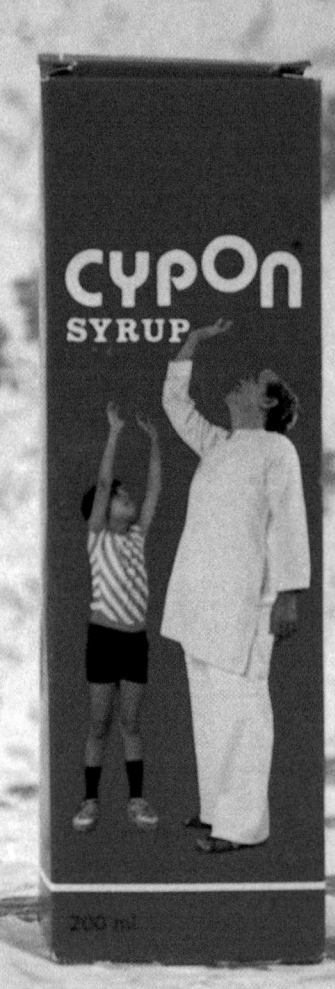

Cypon syrup
Printed cardboard
2 3/8 x 7 7/8 in. (6 x 20 cm)
New Delhi, February 2001
Nothing on the box says what kind of illness this medicine is supposed to cure, so a doctor's prescription is essential. We made inquiries and discovered it is intended to stimulate the appetite, and consequently to increase the patient's growth.

Ora-sore
Printed cardboard
2 3/8 x 3 7/8 x 4 3/4 in. (6 x 10 x 12 cm)
Delhi, February 2001
The eloquence of this design would convince the most hopeless. This gel relieves and heals oral ulcers. The brand is not widely known, and the product, perhaps Ayurvedic, is no doubt made and distributed locally.

Dabur Shilajeet capsules
1 3/4 x 2 1/2 in. (4.5 x 6.5 cm)
These capsules promise to "sustain the force of youth."

Box of kohl
Printed cardboard
3/4 x 2 1/2 in. (2 x 6.5 cm)
Ajmer, January 2001
The use of kohl is not purely aesthetic: It is applied to children's eyes because its antiseptic properties help protect them from the host of infections that may beset them on the way to school. Kohl is also used to make a black mark on babies, usually behind an ear, to keep off the evil eye: This deliberate and obvious little flaw makes them imperfect, disfigured, and thus less likely to arouse the jealousy of the djinns.

Flasks of floral essences
4 3/4 x 1 3/4 in. (diameter) (12 x 4.5 cm)
Mumbai, Mohamed Ali Road, April 2003
Magic or Gulitan Rose, unabashedly: These
essences, spread through the hair or over
the body, bear names full of promise. Indians,
especially Muslims, are great alchemists when
it comes to essential oils and other substances
alleged to increase attractiveness. What is
more, they know how to apply them skillfully.

Box of eyewash
Printed cardboard
1 5/8 x 2 3/8 in. (4 x 6 cm)
Jaipur, Tripolia Bazaar, February 1999
Dust and pollution wreak havoc on the most
sensitive eyes. The drawing speaks volumes.

Kuf Kuf
Bottle of cough syrup
Glass and plastic
3 1/8 x 1 3/8 in. (diameter) (8 x 3.5 cm)
Jaipur, Tripolia Bazaar, February 1999

Images are still a legitimate and important means of conveying a message, and those on medicine-bottle labels are no exception to this rule. As we see here, an effective graphic design may substitute for the instructions. Reinforced by a highly eloquent onomatopoeia, this package of cough syrup promises everyone, even the most illiterate, prompt improvement in health. Here, the individual expressing his temporary discomfort looks, it seems to us, rather *Simpsons*-esque.

Rhumasyl ointment
Printed cardboard
1 3/4 x 4 7/8 in. (4.5 x 12.5 cm)
Delhi, February 2001
The highly realistic anatomical illustration decorating this bottle clearly indicates the target of this ointment:
It promises to relieve all kinds of pains of the muscles and joints. This Ayurvedic preparation is made
from plants and uses an age-old recipe, but the packaging in no way refers to a tradition freighted with
spirituality—there are no New Age packaging or spiritualistic pseudo-explanations here, because the
classical and serious imagery of anatomy is still requisite.

बिजली बिजली

फ़्लग फ़्लग

तार तार

बल्ब बल्ब

बत्ती बत्ती

लालटेन लालटेन

माला माला

रौशनी रौशनी

Colors — Plugs — Wire — Bulbs —

Christmas-tree lights — Lighting

Lightbulbs and other electrical accessories are a source of endless fascination in India. Specialized storekeepers make a good living, even in villages. Colored or ornamental designs are as commonly found as regular lightbulbs are. When you drive around at night, you see a number of shops that display multicolored designs and strings of Christmas-tree lights. These bulbs give out a warm, delicate light; they are a little bit like candles. They serve as household night lights, and are especially popular for lighting temples and public or personal altars.

At evening marriages, very solemn individuals wearing strings of lights on their heads and connected by electrical wires to a purring generator surround the procession: the husband on his white mare, his veiled wife walking behind, friends and relatives dressed up in their finery. These walking chandeliers are disappearing today, however, giving way to large white or colored neon lights, but the spectacle is still striking.

Production of lightbulbs in India does not seem to obey the same industrial principles as observed elsewhere. They're often produced by a network of small workshops that make them under the aegis of a big national brand such as Lakshmi. Safety is still a secondary concern, and the establishment of standards seems a distant possibility. Quality is hit or miss, and any electrical-goods dealer worthy of the name will, of his own accord, test all the lightbulbs the client picks out.

It was almost 2 A.M., but Gustad was not sleepy. Mixing memory and sorrow, he thought fondly of the old days. At last, he dipped the nib in the ink bottle and began. . . . As he wrote the salutation, the power returned. The bulb blazed over the dining table. After hours of darkness, the harsh electric light flooded the room insolently from corner to corner. He switched it off and resumed writing by the kerosene lamp.

Rohinton Mistry, *Such a Long Journey*
New York: Vintage, 1992

Lamps — Sockets

खतरा

७८०००   वोल्ट्स

78000   VOLTS

DANGER

Sign
Enameled metal
10 x 7 in. (25.5 x 18 cm)
Mumbai, Chor Bazaar, 2003
Is India electrically overloaded? Yes, if you believe this enameled sign, which boasts of 78,000 volts, and if you look at traffic in the streets of Mumbai, or at the undulating walk of the stars of recent Bollywood films.

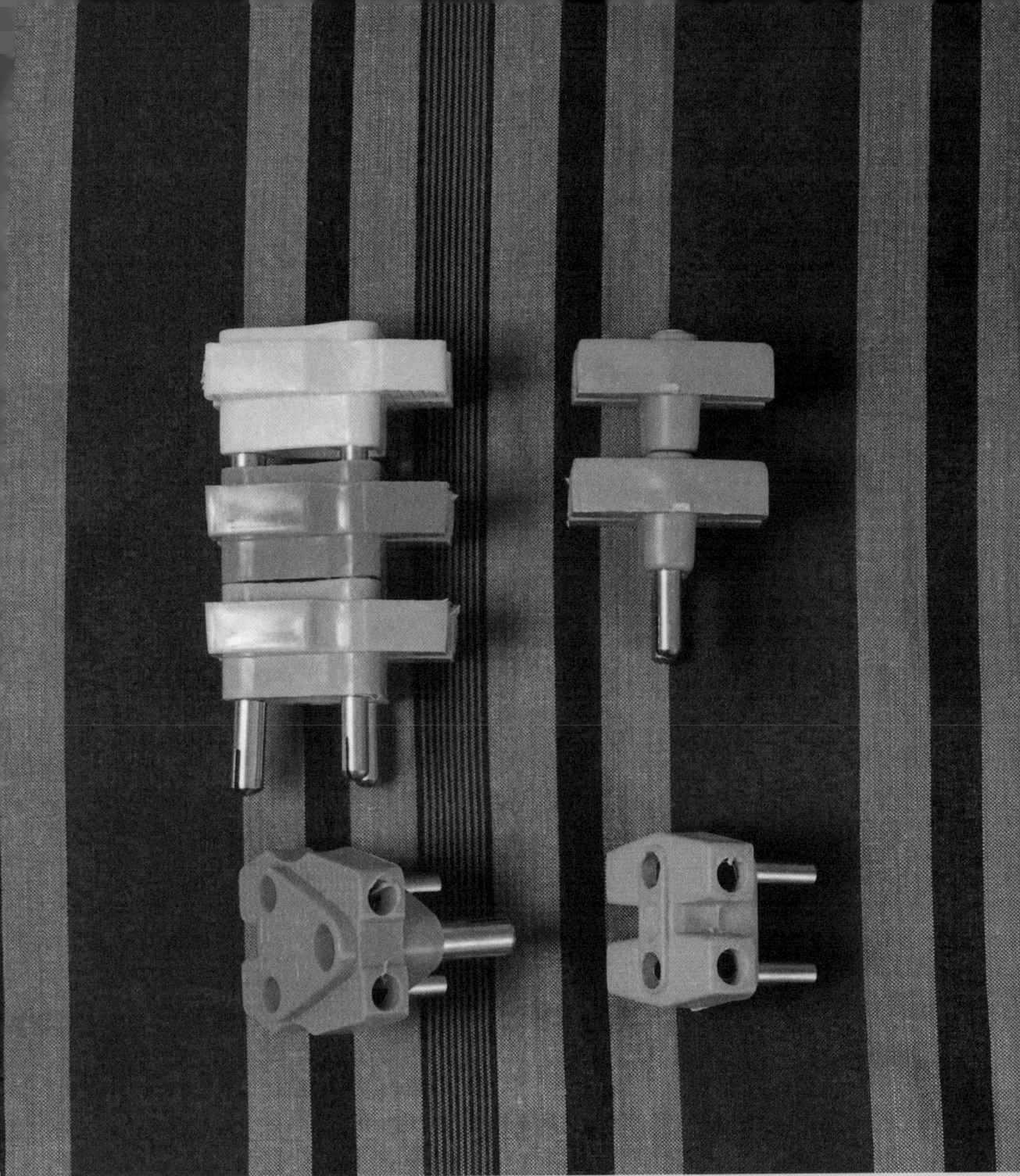

Multiple plugs
Metal and plastic
2 x 1³/₈ x ³/₄ in. (5 x 3.5 x 2 cm)
Mumbai, Mangaldas Road, April 2003
Several electrical standards exist in India. The grounded plug was introduced by the British.

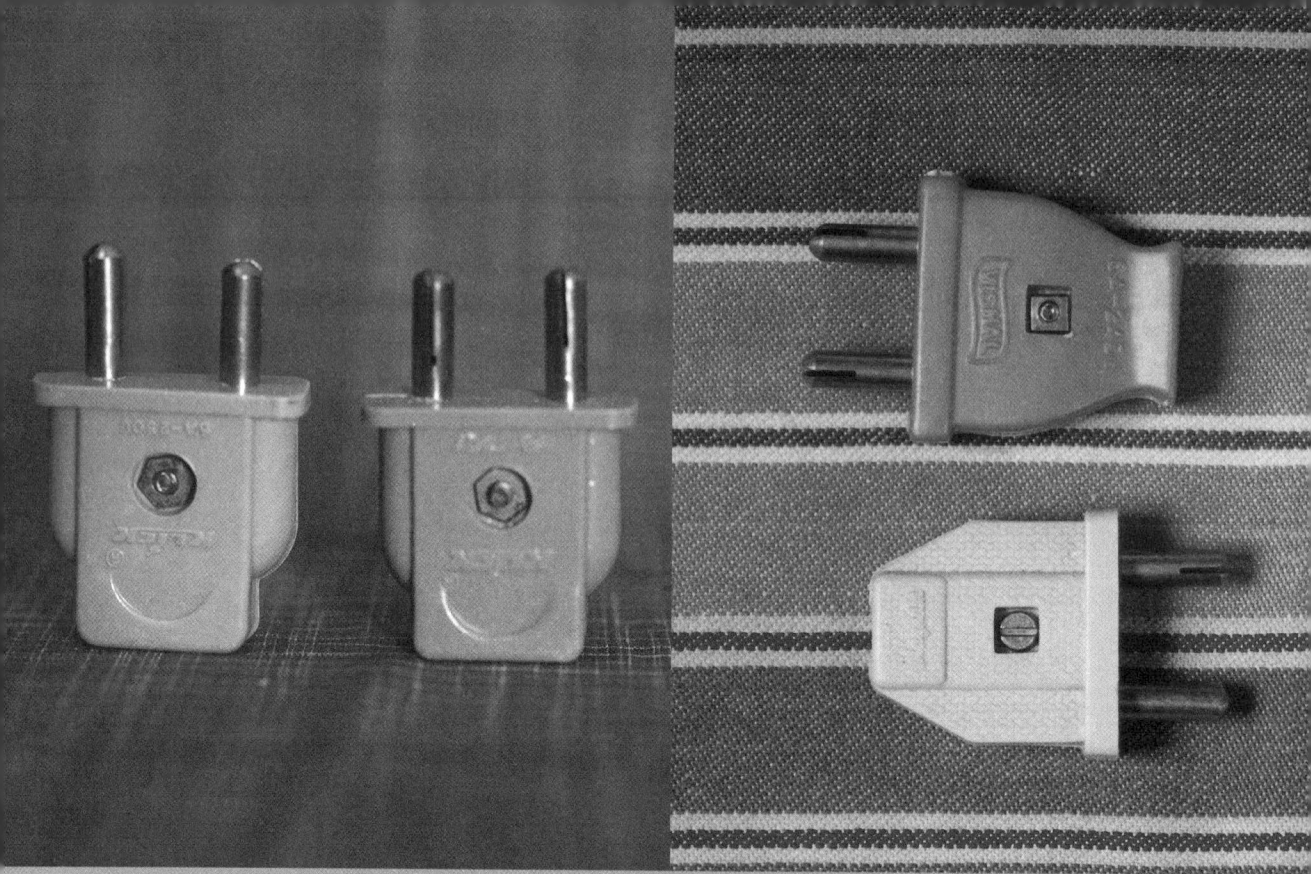

Electrical plugs
Pink and gray plastic, metal
1 3/4 x 1 3/8 x 5/8 in. (4.5 x 3.5 x 1.5 cm)
Bangalore, February 1999
Indian electrical plugs don't try to blend in with the decor, and they unabashedly display the most
appealing colors, subtle or bright.

Plugs
Beige and blue plastic, metal
1 3/4 x 1 3/8 x 5/8 in. (4.5 x 3.5 x 1.5 cm)
Mumbai, Mangaldas Road, April 2003
Textural effects in the plastic and technical information decorate this example.

Mr. Kapur tore away the protective padding and held up the custom-designed prop. Made of a round
light bulb, it was the bright red colour of a new cricket ball, with rows of stitches painted along its
circumference to resemble the seam. . . . The transparent string escaped Yezad's fingers. The bulb
fell to the floor and shattered.

"Oh no!" Mr. Kapur jumped back to avoid the shards of glass.

Yezad's hands were shaking as he came down the ladder. . . . Distressed as Yezad was, he knew
Mr. Kapur needed to be pacified.

"Maybe we can put in a regular bulb for the time being," he suggested. . . .

The peon swept up the bits of red glass that were scattered around like drops of blood. . . . When
they were through, Mr. Kapur inserted the bulb in the socket and started the motor. . . . But the
substitute bulb's thin yellow light had jaundiced the mood.

Rohinton Mistry, *Family Matters*
New York: Vintage, 2003

Vishal plug
Metal and plastic
Varying dimensions
Mumbai, Mangaldas Road, April 2003
Neither the pearlescent of the plastic nor the color are thought to bespeak a weak technical presentation.

"Thief" socket and plug
Black and white plastic
1 3/4 x 1 3/8 x 2 in. (4.5 x 3.5 x 5 cm)
Mumbai, Mangaldas Road, April 2003
These devices give you an idea of household wiring in India. Sometimes a single outlet serves all the lighting needs of three rooms. By way of many extension cords, and, thanks to multifunctional sockets and plugs, people manage to bring electricity to where it is needed without much concern for safety.

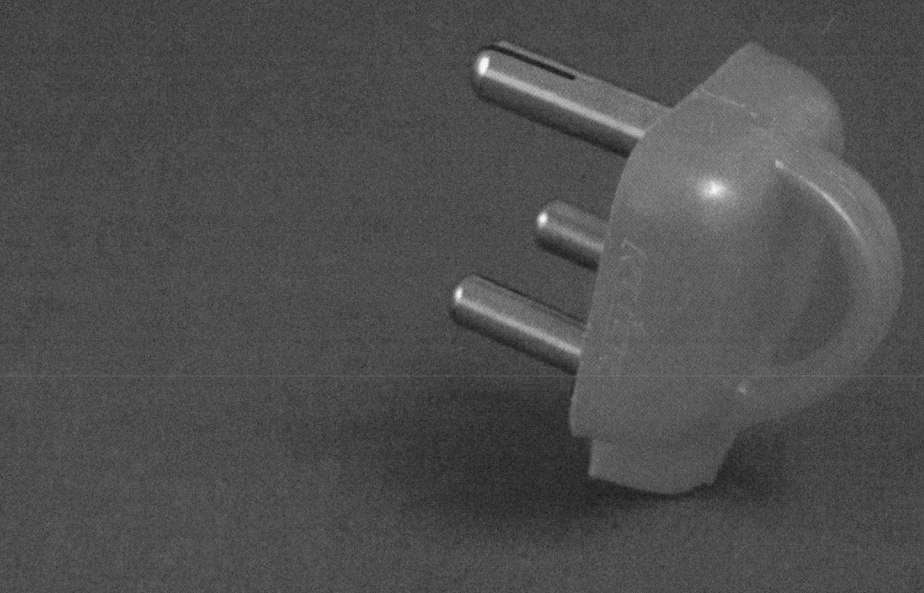

Electrical plug
Plastic and metal
2 x 2 x 2 3/8 in. (5 x 5 x 6 cm)
Bangalore, February 1999
Note, in addition to the ergonomic concerns signaled by the addition of the little handle, which allows
unplugging the cord from the wall without danger, the brilliant orange color.

Unrated lightbulb
Glass, metal, and paint
2 3/4 x 2 in. (diameter) (7 x 5 cm)
Mumbai, Mangaldas Road, April 2003
If you look carefully at this lightbulb, you will see that it is far from spherical. It was nevertheless
purchased in an electrical-goods store, and with no offer of a discount. In India, if an object is able to
fulfill its function, there is no question of selling it at a reduced cost, whether it is misshapen or not.

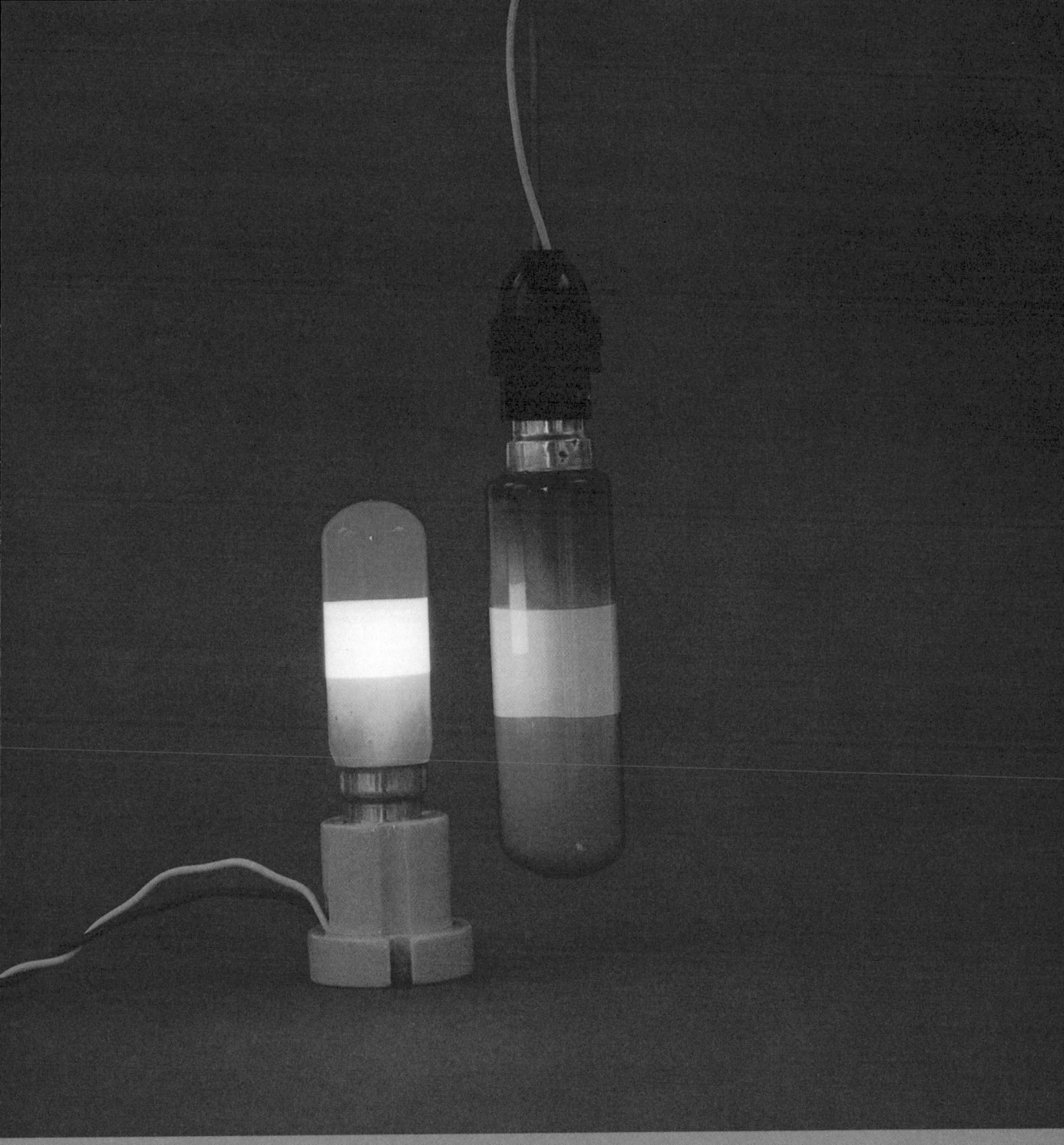

Flag lightbulbs
Glass, metal, and paint
Small bulb: $3\,^1/_2$ x $1\,^3/_8$ in. (diameter) (9 x 3.5 cm)
Large bulb: $5\,^1/_8$ x 2 in. (diameter) (13 x 5 cm)
Mumbai, Mangaldas Road, April 2003

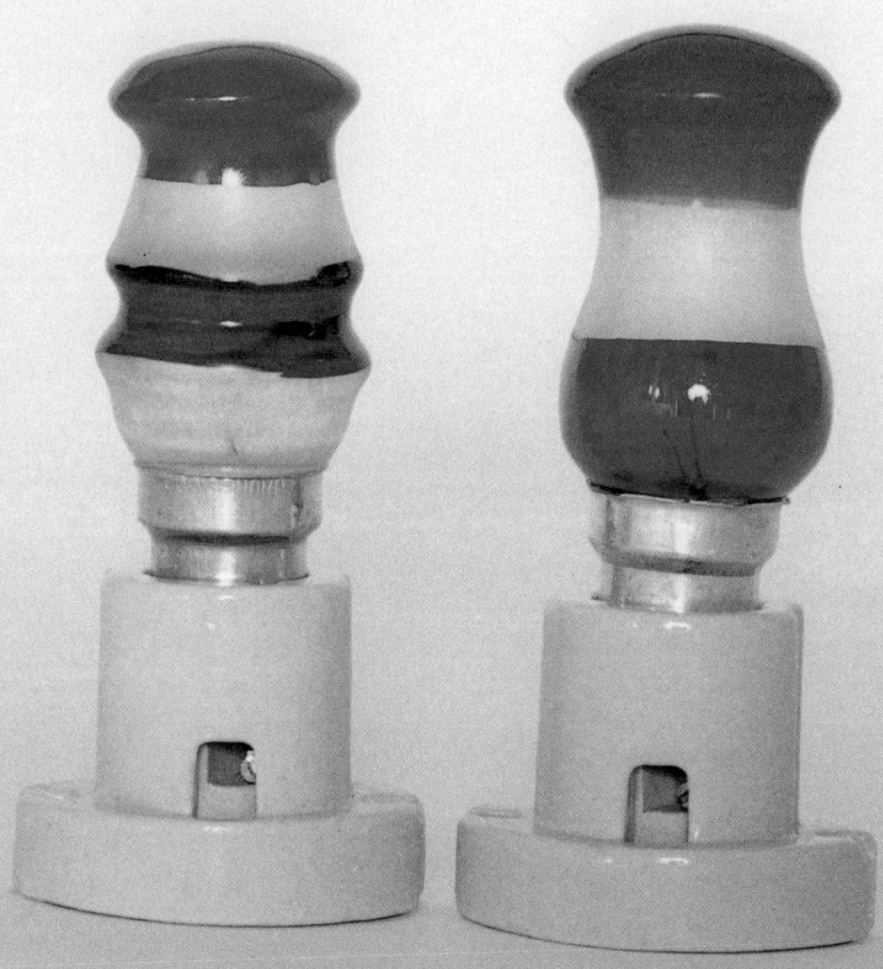

Three-colored lightbulbs
Glass, metal, and paint
3 7/8 x 2 in. (10 x 5 cm)
Jodhpur, February 2001
The colors of the national flag embellish a multitude of different styles—simple or tortuous tubular forms, opaque or transparent—and in various sizes. All the same, the more unusual and the more fragile among them, like the "fluted sausage" and the "mushroom," are admittedly becoming rare in large cities. These lightbulbs are sold near where they were produced.

Green display samples
Glass, metal, and paint
Varying dimensions
Mumbai, Mangaldas Road, April 2003
The incandescent filaments of these bulbs shine throughout India in towns and villages, bearing a warm
light and brightening the most dreary of places.

Flame bulb
Glass and metal
3 1/2 x 1 3/8 in. (diameter) (9 x 3.5 cm)
Mumbai, Mangaldas Road, April 2003
This lightbulb dimly illuminates temples and alters with its little mystic flame. The socket, like this one, is invariably pink.

234

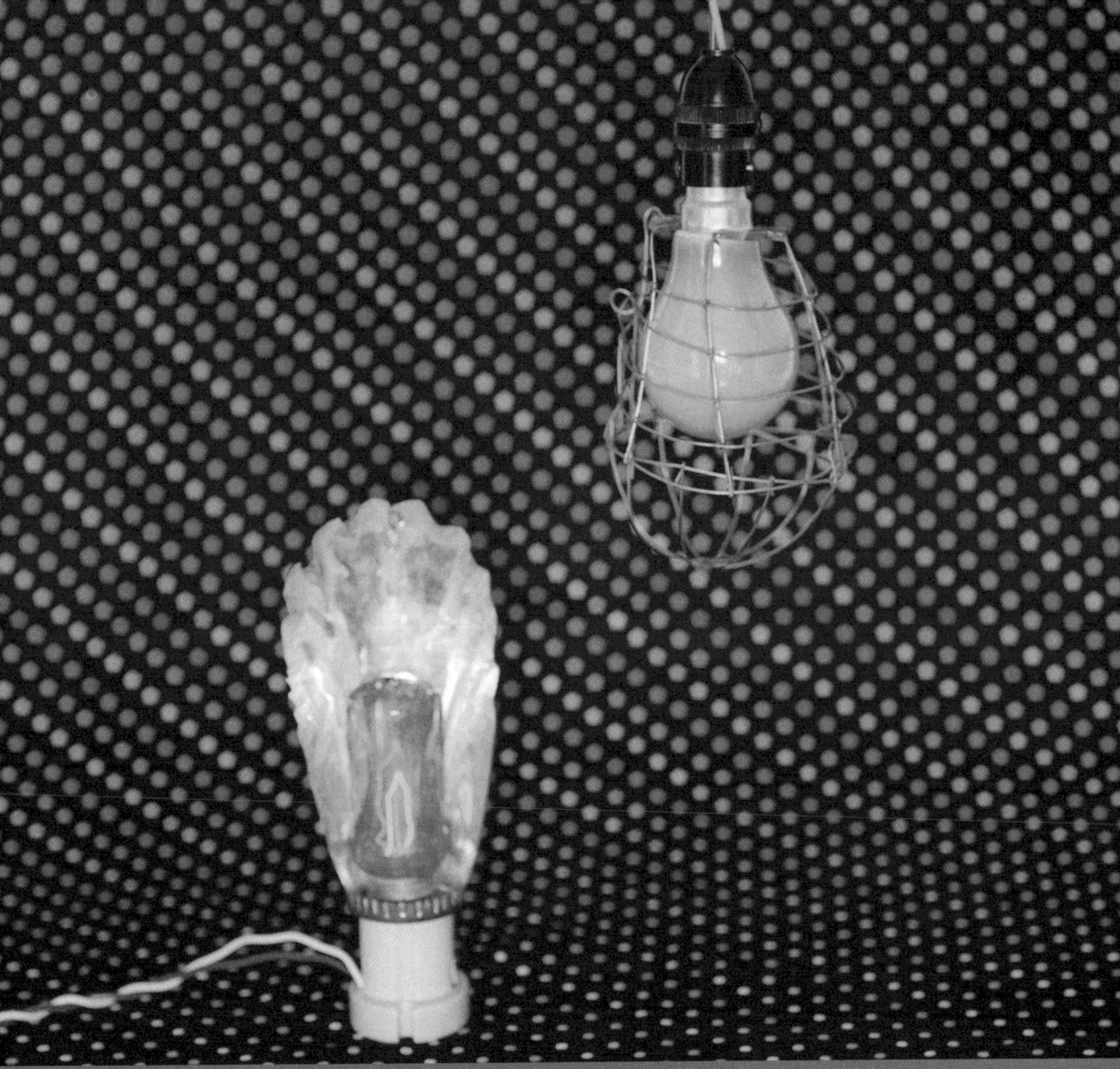

Bulb cage
Zinc-plated iron wire
6 3/4 x 5 1/8 in. (diameter) (17 x 13 cm)
Jaipur, Tripolia Bazaar, February 1999

Reflector
Plated steel
7 1/8 x 4 3/8 in. (18 x 11 cm)
Jaipur, Tripolia Bazaar, February 1999
Like the cover of a mechanic's lamp, this bulb cage protects the fragile globe of glass from damage, but it is especially useful in preventing theft. It is fixed to the socket between two rings that screw together, and a little padlock slides into the loop that closes the cage. In fact, when the lamp lights a public or semipublic place (such as a corridor), it is preferable to lock it securely, so as not to arouse greed. The reflector, on the other hand, lets you focus the light in any direction.

Red and orange sample lights
Glass, metal, and paint
Varying dimensions
Mumbai, Mangaldas Road, April 2003
Near the end of his speech, he gave a hand signal to someone waiting in the wings with a walkie-talkie.
Seconds later, colored lights hidden in the floral proscenium arch began to flash powerfully enough to
compete with the midday sun. The audience was impressed. The feeble mandatory clapping for the
member of parliament's speech now became genuine applause for the visual display.

Rohinton Mistry, *A Fine Balance*
New York: Vintage, 1997

Scratched bulbs
Glass, metal, and paint
2 5/8 x 1 3/4 in. (diameter) (6.7 x 4.5 cm)
Mumbai, Mangaldas Road, April 2003
Imagination and innovation are always a good thing. These spherical bulbs, covered with opaque black paint scratched away to reveal colored decorations, have just appeared on the market.

Christmas-tree lights
Glass, metal, plastic
78 3/4 in. (2 m)
Jodhpur, February 2001
The enchanting grace of this string of lights is unfortunately due to the extreme thinness of the wire, the flimsiness of the soldering, and the fragility of the bulbs.

String of electric lights, mounted on cloth
118 1/8 x 1 1/8 x 1 1/8 in. (3 m x 3 cm x 3 cm)
Mumbai, Mangaldas Road, April 2003
This string of lights was used in most exterior illuminations, whether to celebrate marriages or to decorate temples or hotels. Thanks to the cloth band, it's easy to roll out in trees and nail to buildings. It was, in its time, a great step forward in safety, because the bulbs are screwed into a real socket instead of just being soldered to the wire with a little drop of lead alloy. In the recent past, bulbs were colored by wrapping each one in a little piece of red, pink, orange, yellow, green, or blue cellophane attached to the socket with a rubber band. As a sign of the changing times, a real manufactured product now is supplanting this handcrafted work (which costs nothing, except time): Now, as an option, little bulb covers in transparent and colored plastic, which fulfill the same function and stand up to the rain and sun much better, are available.

Lightbulbs
Glass, metal, and paint
5^7/$_8$ x 3^1/$_8$ in. (15 x 8 cm)
Mumbai, Mangaldas Road, February 1999, February 2000 and April 2003
This large bulb, which seems to have been produced under license from Philips, comes in red, yellow, green, turquoise, and white. It has been spotted only in a particular store in Mumbai, and we searched for it everywhere, because it has two attractions: color, and a power of 60 watts.

Lightbulbs
Blue, white, and transparent glass, and metal
6 1/8 x 2 3/4 in. (diameter) (15.5 x 7 cm)
Mumbai, Mangaldas Road, April 2003
These lightbulbs are powerful (200 watts) but rather fragile. The opaque white bulb is a mercury bulb, and it lights in fits and starts. The blue one produces black light, while the transparent one is often used to light displays set up in the street after dark.

Two-colored lightbulbs
Glass, metal, and paint
3 7/8 x 2 1/5 in. (diameter) (10 x 6.5 cm)
Mumbai, Mangaldas Road, April 2003
Indians like to enclose these bulbs in a white paper lamp shade so that the different layers of color are
especially visible. As with many other designs, the color is applied by hand by dipping the bulb in lacquers
of different colors, one after the other.

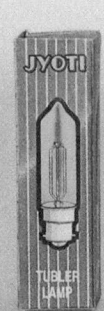

Double-socket lightbulb
Glass and metal
6 3/4 x 1 5/8 in. (diameter) (17 x 4 cm)
Mysore, February 1998
With two sockets, this lightbulb is resolutely out of the ordinary. We could find no lamp to fit it in the shop in which we found it. Despite its eccentricity, this model seemingly did not find the success it sought: We never saw it anywhere else.

Boxes of light bulbs
Printed and silk-screened cardboard
2 3/4–5 7/8 x 1 1/8–3 7/8 x 1 1/8–3 7/8 in. (7–15 x 3–10 x 3–10 cm)
Mumbai, Mangaldas Road, April 2003
These packages are worthy of their contents: brightly colored, delicate, and graphically irresistible. The color of the bulb is unfortunately rarely indicated, so that you have to open all the boxes to check, which is sometimes rather tedious.

Miniature lightbulbs
Glass and metal
$3/4 \times 5/8$ and $3/4$ in. (2 x 1.5 and 2 cm)
Ajmer, February 2001

The charm of these little bulbs, which look like bubbles of light, hides a degree of danger. They're hooked together in a string, each attached to the others by their wires, without any insulation. Each of them is rated at 5 volts, and you have to join together forty-four to plug them in, because the voltage rate in India is 220 volts. If one of them comes undone, the others burn out. When they work, however, they make magnificent necklaces of light reserved, unfortunately, for the portraits of ancestors or divinities hanging from walls.

Desk lamps
Painted metal, plastic, cardboard, and cement
4 3/8 x 5 7/8 x 11 3/4 in. (11 x 15 x 30 cm)
Jaipur, Tripolia Bazaar, February 2001; Delhi, Kinari Bazaar, February 2002
These lamps are found throughout India, but today they are becoming more and more rare. The metal from which they are made is thin, and they're so light that their stability has to be ensured by a piece of cement cast within the base. A little piece of cardboard rolled around the socket provides insulation. Scratches and runs in the paint are common, and seem inherent to the object. They're very practical.

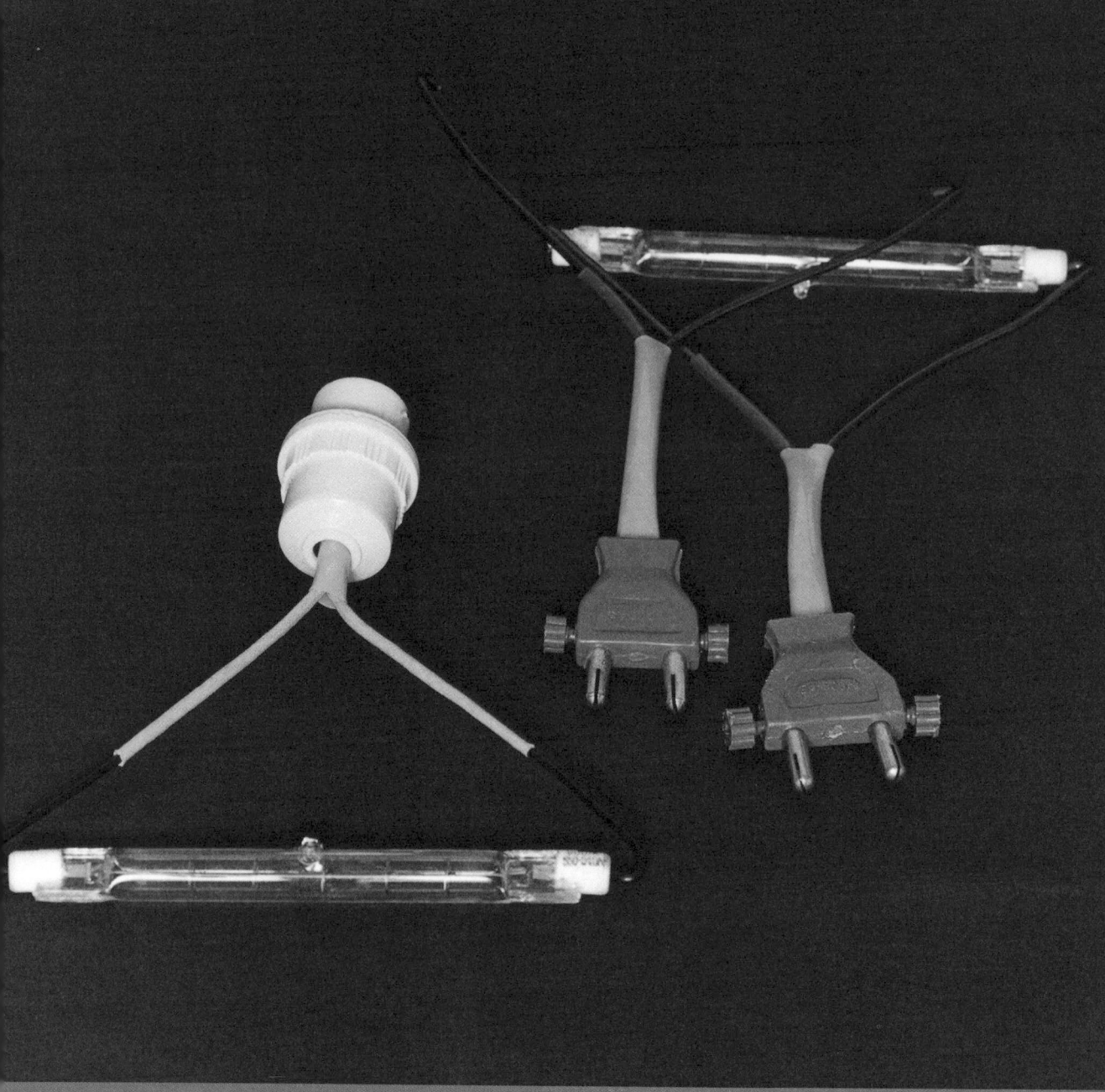

Electrical contraptions
Plastic and metal
5 $^7/_8$ x 4 $^3/_4$ in. (15 x12 cm)
Mumbai, April 2003
These lamps clearly illustrate the lack of safety regulations that governs the Indian marketplace. They are commonly sold in the streets and come in two versions: socket or plug. The test we made, enchanted with our purchase and impatient to see it at work, was conclusive: a blinding flash of light, the socket melted, and the fuses blown. No doubt we bought a bad one, because many street peddlers still sell them. As for us, we won't buy any others, which is too bad, because the plugs unscrew from the outside without a screwdriver, which is very handy with makeshift wiring.

Flashlight
Metal and plastic
7 x 2 in. (diameter) (18 x 5 cm)
Nawalgarh, February 2002
This device unabashedly displays its guts, allowing for easy diagnosis in case of failure.

Display of lamps
Delhi, Kinari Bazaar, March 2003
This is a fairly typical display, although, depending on the year and the style, shapes and colors change.

248

A few years ago, for example, matte colors—red, khaki green, dark blue, and gray—predominated.
Later, colors became metallic, or red, as here.

Originally published in France by Éditions du Seuil in 2004
under the title *100% Indian*.

Copyright © 2004 by Éditions du Seuil
Photographs copyright © Catherine Geel
Original ISBN 2-02-062882-1

English translation copyright © 2005 by Éditions du Seuil.
All rights reserved. No part of this book may be reproduced in any
form without written permission from the publisher.

Library of Congress Cataloging-in-Publication Data available.

ISBN: 2-02-069420-4

Manufactured in Spain.

English translation by Jack Hawkes
Book design by Valerie Gautier
English cover design by Vanessa Dina
English typesetting by Janis Reed

Distributed in Canada by Raincoast Books
9050 Shaughnessy Street, Vancouver, British Columbia V6P 6E5

10 9 8 7 6 5 4 3 2 1

Chronicle Books LLC
85 Second Street, San Francisco, California 94105

www.chroniclebooks.com

हार्दिक धन्यवाद

We are deeply grateful to the following people for their help and confidence:

The Cultural Service of the French Embassy to India

Jérôme Neutres, cultural attaché to New Delhi

Djallal Gérard Heuzé, research director, Centre National de la Recherche Scientifique (National Scientific Research Center); member of the Centre d'Etudes et de Recherches Internationales (Center for International Research and Study) and the Centre d'Etudes de l'Inde et de l'Asie du Sud (Center for Indian and Southeast Asian Studies)

Max-Jean Zins, research director at the Centre National de la Recherche Scientifique (National Scientific Research Center) and the Centre d'Etudes et de Recherches Internationales (Center for International Research and Study), and a member of the Centre d'Etudes de l'Inde et de l'Asie du Sud (Center for Indian and Southeast Asian Studies)

Saleem Bhatri, designer, who proofread all our captions and gave us priceless information

Valentina Pilia, who measured all the objects and very efficiently helped Catherine Geel with the photography

Myriam Rassiwala

Radhika Jha

Rohit Khattar

Armita David

Yuki Ellias

Doris Jugganadum of the Route des Indes

Stéphanie Geel

Agathe and Desmond Lazaro

Sigolène and Christophe Prébois